AA Phrasebook
GERMAN

AA

English edition prepared by First Edition Translations.
Additional phrases provided by Quarto Translations.

Produced by AA Publishing
First published in 1995 as Wat & Hoe Duits,
© Kosmos Uitgevers – Utrecht/Antwerpen

First edition 1997
Second edition 2006
Third edition 2008
This revised edition © AA Media Limited 2013
Reprinted 2013 and 2014

A CIP catalogue record for this book is available from the British Library.

Published by AA Publishing (a trading name of AA Media Limited, whose registered office is Fanum House, Basingstoke, Hampshire RG21 4EA. Registered number 06112600).

Printed in China by Leo Paper Products.

ISBN 978-0-7495-7414-7

A05278

Visit AA Publishing at theAA.com/shop

Contents

5 On the road 67–83

6 Public transport 84–95

7 Overnight accommodation 96–107

8 Money matters 108–111

9 Communications 112–118

Introduction

● **Welcome to the AA's German phrasebook**.

Key sections

This book is divided into 15 themed sections and starts with a
pronunciation table (see opposite), which gives you the phonetic
spelling to all the words and phrases you'll need to know for your trip,
This is followed by a **grammar guide** (page 8), which will help you
construct basic sentences in your chosen language. At the back of the
book (page 163 onwards), you'll find an extensive **word list**.

Finding the right phrase

Throughout the book you'll come across boxes featuring a 🔲 symbol.
These are designed to help you if you can't understand what your
listener is saying to you. Hand the book over to them and encourage
them to point to the appropriate answer to the question you are asking.

Other tinted boxes in the book – this time without the symbol – give
alphabetical listings of themed words with their English translations
beside them.

For extra clarity, we have put all English words and phrases in black,
foreign language terms in colour and phonetic pronunciations in italic.

Enjoy your trip

This phrasebook covers all the subjects you are likely to encounter
during the course of your visit, from reserving a room for the night to
ordering food and drink and what to do if your car breaks down or you
lose your money. With over 2,000 commonly used words and phrases
at your fingertips, you'll be able to get by in all situations. Let this book
become your passport to a secure and enjoyable trip.

Pronunciation table

The pronunciation provided should be read as if it were English, bearing in mind the following main points:

Vowels

a	is like **ar**	*ar*	as in **Kater**	*karter*
	or the **u** in cup	*u*	as in **Tasse**	*tusser*
ä	is like **ay** in may	*ay*	as in **spät**	*shpayt*
	or **e** in edible	*e*	as in **hält**	*helt*
e	is like **ay** in may	*ay*	as in **Nebel**	*naybel*
	or **e** in edible	*e*	as in **Mensch**	*mensh*
	or **air** in fair	*air*	as in **Schmerz**	*shmairts*
i	is like **i** in lick	*i*	as in **Mitte**	*mitter*
o	is like **oa** in boat	*oa*	as in **Motor**	*moator*
	or **o** in lock	*o*	as in **Socke**	*zokker*
ö	is like **u** in fur	*oe*	as in **öffnen**	*oefnen*
u	is like **oo** in ooze	*oo*	as in **Kur**	*koor*
ü	is like **ue** in cue	*ue*	as in **fünf**	*fuenf*

Consonants

Consonants are mainly as in English except for

g	like **g** in great	*g*	as in **Gigant**	*gigant*
j	like **y** in yes	*y*	as in **ja**	*yar*
s	when at beginning of word, like **z**	*z*	as in **Seife**	*zaifer*
v	like **f** in fish	*f*	as in **Volk**	*folk*
w	like **v** in vole	*v*	as in **Wagen**	*vargen*
z	like **ts** in cats	*ts*	as in **zwölf**	*tsvoelf*

At the end of a word **b**, **d**, and **g** change in sound to **p**, **t** and **k** respectively. The symbol **ß** (es-tset) stands for **ss** and is rare.

Some combinations of letters

au is pronounced *ow* as in cow; **eu** and **äu** are pronounced *oy* as in boy; **ie** is pronounced *ee* as in feet; **ei** and **ai** are pronounced as *ai* in Thai; **ch** is like *ch* in loch but rendered in the pronunciation as *kh*; **qu** is pronounced *kv*; **sp** and **st** at the start of a word are pronounced *shp* and *sht*; **sch** is also pronounced *sh*.

Stress

Usually on the leading syllable or on the stem (root) of the word, e.g. **stehen** (to stand) is stressed *shtayen*, **verstehen** (to understand) is stressed fair*shtayen*.

Basic grammar

1 Nouns

German nouns are divided into three types, known as genders: masculine, feminine, and neuter. German also has a system of cases for its nouns, four in number, and referred to in English as Nominative (for the subject), Accusative (for the object), Genitive (the possessive case), and Dative (the **to** or **for** case).

2 Definite article (the)

	Masculine	Feminine	Neuter
Nominative	**der**	**die**	**das**
Accusative	**den**	**die**	**das**
Genitive	**des**	**der**	**des**
Dativedem	**der**	**dem**	

The plural is the same for all:

Nominative	**die**
Accusative	**die**
Genitive	**der**
Dative	**den**

3 Indefinite article (a or an)

	Masculine	Feminine	Neuter
Nominative	**ein**	**eine**	**ein**
Accusative	**einen**	**eine**	**ein**
Genitive	**eines**	**einer**	**eines**
Dative	**einem**	**einer**	**einem**

Note that when masculine and neuter nouns are in the possessive (genitive) case, they have an **s** at the end, not totally unlike English; **der Hund des Mannes** (the man's dog).

4 Plurals

Nouns can be rather erratic. There are a few basic principles: Nouns ending in -**keit** and -**heit** and -**ung** add the letters -**en** to form the plural. **Neuheit** (novelties) becomes **Neuheiten** (novelties); **Sehenswürdigkeit** (something worth seeing, tourist attraction) becomes **Sehenswürdigkeiten** (tourist attractions); **Hoffnung** (hope) becomes **Hoffnungen** (hopes). Also, as a general rule, if a word ends in an -**e**, assume you can make the plural by adding an **n**; **Witwe** (widow) becomes **Witwen** (widows). In the case of masculine and neuter nouns making the plural not infrequently involves making a change in the vowels within the word as well as adding an ending. Try adding the sound -**e** or **er** to the singular form, and you should be able to put the meaning across.In the plural form of the Dative case, all nouns add an -**n**. **Berg** (mountain) is a masculine noun (**der Berg**), and becomes **Berge** in the plural (mountains); on the mountains becomes **auf den Bergen**.

5 Adjectives

Adjectives come in front of the noun. There is an arrangement for making the adjective agree with the noun if it is used without any article (no **the** or **a**), which is basically like **der**, **die**, **das**; Black thing, for example, is **schwarzes Ding**, pretty woman is **schöne Frau**, big dog is **grosser Hund**. If we place an article before the adjective, things are easier; the black thing is **das schwarze Ding**, the pretty woman is **die schöne Frau**, the big dog is **der grosse Hund**. Of the black thing; **des schwarzen Dings**. Of the pretty woman; **der schönen Frau**. Of the big dog; **des grossen Hunds**. (You may also hear **Dinges** and **Hundes**.)

6 Adverbs

Adverbs are essentially the same in German as adjectives; in other words, he does it well is **er tut es gut** (*err toot ez goot*), which means he does it good. Know one and you know the other.

7 Pronouns

	First (I)	Second (you)	Third (he)	(she)	(it)
Nominative	**ich**	**Sie**	**er**	**sie**	**es**
Accusative	**mich**	**Sie**	**ihn**	**sie**	**es**
Dative	**mir**	**Ihnen**	**ihm**	**ihr**	**ihm**

The forms for the plural, they, are **sie**, **sie**, **ihnen**. Accordingly, he sees me becomes **er sieht mich**; she sees him: **sie sieht ihn**. I see it: **ich sehe es**. The dative case is the case which occurs mostly if prepositions are involved (with, by, from, for example).

There is also a form for you which is used for close friends, talking to very small children, and animals; this is **Du**, and should be avoided unless you are really sure of your ground. There is a plural form of this, **ihr**. The usual word for you is **Sie** (pronounced *zee*), and when written always has a capital letter for its forms, to distinguish it from the forms for they.

8 Verbs

German verbs, like English verbs, come in two kinds, traditionally referred to as strong and weak. Weak verbs are the regular ones, and are easy; strong verbs are irregular, and can really only be learnt. An example of a weak verb in English is to walk; I walk, I walked, I have walked. An example of a strong verb is to swim; I swim, I swam, I have swum. The weak verbs make their forms which indicate action in the past in a regular way, too: I was loving is **ich liebte**; he was loving **er liebte**; we/you/they were loving: **Wir/Sie/sie liebten**. The strong verbs change the vowel in the main part of the verb: **ich schwimme** becomes **ich schwamm** (I swam).

A German weak verb looks like this:

Lieben	To love
ich liebe	I love (also doubles up for I am loving, I do love)
(**Du liebst**)	(you love; this is the very friendly form)
er/sie/es liebt	he/she/it loves
wir lieben	we love
Sie lieben	you love
sie lieben	they love

The other difference between weak and strong verbs occurs in the past participle. Weak verbs are regular in their past participles; add the letters **ge-** to the front, and replace the -**en** at the end of the verb by a -**t**. **Lieben** (to love) gives us a past participle **gelebt** (loved); **spielen** (to play) gives **gespielt** (played), and so on.

Strong verbs do not make this change; e.g. **schwimmen** gives us **geschwommen** (swum), **sehen** (to see) gives us **gesehen**.

A quick look at the verbs "to have" and "to be":

Haben	To have
ich habe	I have
(**Du hast**)	(you have; very friendly form)
er/sie/es hat	he/she/it has
wir/Sie/sie haben	we/you/they have

Sein	To be
ich bin	I am
(Du bist)	(you are; very friendly form)
er/sie/es ist	he/she/it has
wir/Sie/sie sind	we/you/they are

In principle, the past form I have (done something) is created by using the relevant part of **haben** for verbs which have an object (I have seen him: **ich habe ihn gesehen**; I have done it: **ich habe es getan**), and the relevant parts of sein for verbs which do not have an object (I have swum: **ich bin geschwommen**; I have come: **ich bin gekommen**; I have flown: **Ich bin geflogen**). Bear in mind that, in the past form using have, the past participle comes at the end of the sentence.

9 Prepositions

in means in or into
auf means on or onto
mit means with
zu means to
for means for
bei means with or in the vicinity of (but rarely by)
von means of or from

Most prepositions are associated with the dative case, although some are found with the accusative e.g. **in der Stadt**: IN the town, **in die Stadt**: INTO the town.

1. Useful lists

1.1 Today or tomorrow?

What day is it today?	Welcher Tag ist heute?
	velkher tark ist hoyter?
Today's Monday.	Heute ist Montag.
	hoyter ist moantark
– Tuesday.	Heute ist Dienstag.
	hoyter ist deenstark
– Wednesday.	Heute ist Mittwoch.
	hoyter ist mittvokh
– Thursday.	Heute ist Donnerstag.
	hoyter ist donnerstark
– Friday.	Heute ist Freitag.
	hoyter ist fraitark
– Saturday.	Heute ist Samstag/Sonnabend (S. Germany/ N. Germany).
	hoyter ist zamstark/zonnarbent
– Sunday.	Heute ist Sonntag.
	hoyter ist zonntark
in January	im Januar
	im yannooar
since February	seit Februar
	zait febrooar
in spring	im Frühling
	im fruehling
in summer	im Sommer
	im zommer
in autumn	im Herbst
	im hairpst
in winter	im Winter
	im vinter
2013	zweitausenddreizehn
	tsvaitowzent draitsayn
the 21st century	das einundzwanzigste Jahrhundert
	dass ain oont tsvantsikhster yarhoondert
What's the date today?	Der wievielte ist heute?
	dayr veefeelter ist hoyter?

Today's the 24th.	Heute ist der vierundzwanzigste.	
	hoyter ist dayr fear oont tsvantsikhster	
Monday 3 November 2013	Montag, der 3 November 2013	
	moantark dayr dritter november	
	tsvaitowzendt draitsayn	
Tomorrow is...	Morgen ist...	
	moargen ist	
in the morning	morgens	
	morgens	
midday	mittags (from about 11.30–2pm)	
	mittarks	
in the afternoon	nachmittags	
	nakhmittarks	
in the evening	abends	
	arbents	
at night	nachts	
	nakhts	
this morning	heute morgen	
	hoyter morgen	
this afternoon	heute mittag	
	hoyter mittark	
this evening	heute nachmittag	
	hoyter nakhmittark	
tonight	heute abend	
	hoyter arbent	
last night	letzte nacht	
	letster nakht	
this week	diese Woche	
	deezer vokher	
next month	nächsten Monat	
	nexten moanart	
last year	voriges Jahr	
	forigez yar	
next...	nächste(n)/nächstes...	
	nexter(n)/nextes	
in...days/weeks/months/years	in...Tagen/Wochen/Monaten/Jahren	
	in...targen/vokhen/moanarten/yaren	

...weeks ago	vor...Wochen
	for ... vokhen
day off	der freie Tag
	dayr fraier tark

1.2 Bank holidays

● The most important bank holidays in Germany are the following:

January 1	New Year's Day (Neujahr)
January 6	Epiphany (Hl. Drei Könige)
March/April	Good Friday, Easter and Easter Monday
	(Karfreitag, Ostersonntag und Ostermontag
May 1	May Day (Maifeiertag)
May	Ascension Day (Christi Himmelfahrt)
May/June	Whit Sunday and Whit Monday
	(Pfingstsonntag und Pfingstmontag)
*June	Corpus Christi (Fronleichnam)
*August 15	Feast of the Assumption (Mariä Himmelfahrt)
October 3	Day of German Unity (Tag der deutschen Einheit)
*November 1	All Saints' Day (Allerheiligen)
*November	Buss- und Bettag (day to repent and pray)
	(Wed, variable)
December 25/26	Christmas (Weihnachten)

Most shops, banks and government institutions are closed on these days. The dates marked with an asterisk are Catholic holidays and are mainly celebrated in the south of Germany. On Christmas Eve banks and shops tend to be closed in the afternoon.

1.3 What time is it?

What time is it?	Wie spät ist es?
	vee shpayt ist ez?
It's nine o'clock.	Es ist neun Uhr.
	ez ist noyn ooer
– five past ten.	Es ist fünf nach zehn.
	ez ist fuenf nakh tsayn
– a quarter past eleven.	Es ist Viertel nach elf.
	ez ist feartel nakh elf
– twenty past twelve.	Es ist zwanzig nach zwölf.
	ez ist tsvantsikh nakh tsvoelf
– half past one.	Es ist halb zwei.
	ez ist halp tsvai
– twenty–five to three.	Es ist fünf nach halb drei.
	ez ist fuenf nakh halp drai
– a quarter to four.	Es ist Viertel vor vier.
	ez ist feartel for fear
– ten to five.	Es ist zehn vor fünf.
	ez ist tsayn for fuenf
– twelve noon.	Es ist zwölf.
	ez ist tsvoelf
– midnight.	Es ist Mitternach.t
	ez ist mitternakht
half an hour	eine halbe Stunde
	ainer halber shtoonder
What time?	Um wieviel Uhr?
	oom veefeel ooer?
What time can I come round?	Wann kann ich vorbeikommen?
	vann kann ikh for bai kommen?
At...	Um...
	oom...
After...	Nach…
	nakh...
Before...	Vor…
	for...

Between...and...	Zwischen...und...
	tsvishen...oont...
From...to...	Von... bis...
	fon...biss...
In...minutes.	In...Minuten.
	in...meenooten
– an hour.	In einer Stunde.
	in ainer shtoonder
– ...hours.	In...Stunden.
	In...shtoonden
– a quarter of an hour.	In einer Viertelstunde.
	in ainer feartel shtoonder
– three quarters of an hour.	In einer Dreiviertelstunde.
	in ainer drai feartel shtoonder
early/late	zu früh/spät
	tsoo frue/shpayt
on time	rechtzeitig
	rekht tsaitikh
summertime	(die) Sommerzeit
	(dee) zommer tsait
wintertime	(die) Winterzeit
	(dee) vinter tsait

1.4 One, two, three...

0	null	*nooll*
1	eins	*ains*
2	zwei	*tsvai*
3	drei	*drai*
4	vier	*fear*
5	fünf	*fuenf*
6	sechs	*zekhs*
7	sieben	*zeeben*
8	acht	*akht*
9	neun	*noyn*
10	zehn	*tsayn*

11	elf	*elf*
12	zwölf	*tsvoelf*
13	dreizehn	*draitsayn*
14	vierzehn	*feartsayn*
15	fünfzehn	*fuenftsayn*
16	sechzehn	*zekhtsayn*
17	siebzehn	*zeeptsayn*
18	achtzehn	*akht-tsayn*
19	neunzehn	*noyntsayn*
20	zwanzig	*tsvantsikh*
21	einundzwanzig	*ain oont tsvantsikh*
22	zweiundzwanzig	*tsvai oont tsvantsikh*
30	dreissig	*draissikh*
31	einunddreissig	*ain oont draissikh*
32	zweiunddreissig	*tsvai oont draissikh*
40	vierzig	*feartsikh*
50	fünfzig	*fuenftsikh*
60	sechzig	*zekhtsikh*
70	siebzig	*zeeptsikh*
80	achtzig	*akhttsikh*
90	neunzig	*noyntsikh*
100	hundert	*hoondert*
101	hunderteins	*hoondert ains*
110	hundertzehn	*hoondert tsayn*
120	hundertzwanzig	*hoondert tsvantsikh*
200	zweihundert	*tsvai hoondert*
300	dreihundert	*drai hoondert*
400	vierhundert	*fear hoondert*
500	fünfhundert	*fuenf hoondert*
600	sechshundert	*zekhs hoondert*
700	siebenhundert	*zeeben hoondert*
800	achthundert	*akht hoondert*
900	neunhundert	*noyn hoondert*
1,000	tausend	*towzent*
1,100	tausendeinhundert	*towzent ain hoondert*

2,000	zweitausend	*tsvai towzent*
10,000	zehntausend	*tsayn towzent*
100,000	hunderttausend	*hoondert towzent*
1,000,000	eine Million	*ainer millioan*
1st	erste	*erster*
2nd	zweite	*tsvaiter*
3rd	dritte	*dritter*
4th	vierte	*fearter*
5th	fünfte	*fuenfter*
6th	sechste	*zekhster*
7th	sieb(en)te	*zeeb(en)ter*
8th	achte	*akhter*
9th	neunte	*noynter*
10th	zehnte	*tsaynter*
11th	elfte	*elfter*
12th	zwölfte	*tsvoelfter*
13th	dreizehnter	*draitsaynter*
14th	vierzehnte	*feartsaynter*
15th	fünfzehnte	*fuenftsaynter*
16th	sechzehnte	*zekhtsaynter*
17th	siebzehnte	*zeeptsaynter*
18th	achtzehnte	*akht-tsaynter*
19th	neunzehnte	*noyntsaynter*
20th	zwanzigste	*tsvantsikhster*
21st	einundzwanzigste	*ain oont tsvantsikhster*
22nd	zweiundzwanzigste	*tsvai oont tsvantsikhster*
30th	dreissigste	*draissikhster*
100th	hundertste	*hoondertster*
1,000th	tausendste	*towzentster*
once	einmal	*ainmarl*
twice	zweimal	*tsvaimarl*

double	das Doppelte	*dass doppelter*
triple	das Dreifache	*dass draifakher*
half	die Hälfte	*dee haelfter*
a quarter	ein Viertel	*ain feartel*
a third	ein Drittel	*ain dritel*

a couple, a few, some	ein paar, einige, mehrere
	ain par, ainiger, mayrerer
odd/even	gerade/ungerarde
	gerarder/oongerader
total	(ins)gesamt
	(ins)gezammt

1.5 The weather

Is the weather going to be good/bad?	Wird das Wetter schön/schlecht?
	virt dass vetter shoen/shlekht?
Is it going to get colder/hotter?	Wird es kälter/wärmer?
	virt es kaelter/vaermer?
What temperature is it going to be?	Wieviel Grad wird es?
	veefeel grart virt ez?
Is it going to rain?	Wird es regnen?
	virt ez raygnen?
Is there going to be a storm?	Bekommen wir Sturm?
	bekommen veer shturm?
Is it going to snow?	Wird es schneien?
	virt es shnaien?
Is it going to freeze?	Wird es frieren?
	virt es freeren?
Is the thaw setting in?	Wird es tauen?
	virt es towen?
Is it going to be foggy?	Bekommen wir Nebel?
	bekommen veer naybel?
Is there going to be a thunderstorm?	Wird es ein Gewitter geben?
	virt es ain gevitter gayben?

Bewölkung	**kalt**	**Rückenwind**
cloud	cold	tail wind
Böen	**klar**	**Schnee**
squalls	clear	snow
frisch	**kühl**	**schwül**
chilly	chilly	muggy
(temperature),	**leicht bewölkt**	**sehr heiss**
fresh (wind)	cloudy	scorching hot
Frost	**leichte Bewölkung**	**sonnig**
frost	light clouds	sunny
Glatteis	**mild**	**Sprühregen**
black ice	mild	drizzle
...Grad (unter/über	**nasskalt**	**stark bewölkt**
Null)	cold and damp	overcast
...degrees (above/	**Nebel**	**starke Bewölkung**
below zero)	fog	heavy clouds
Graupel/Hagel	**Orkan**	**Sturm**
hail	hurricane	storm
heiter	**rauh**	**Wind (leichter/**
fine	bleak	**mässiger/starker)**
heiss	**Regenschauer**	light/moderate/strong
hot	shower	wind
Hitzewelle	**Regen(schauer)**	**windig**
heat wave	rain	windy

The weather's changing.	Das Wetter schlägt um.
	dass vetter shlaekt oom
It's cooling down.	Es kühlt sich ab.
	ez kuehlt zikh ap
What's the weather going to be like today/tomorrow?	Was für Wetter wird heute?
	vass fuer vetter virt hoyter?

1.6 Here, there...

See also **5.1 Asking for directions**

here/there	hier/da
	heer/dar
somewhere/nowhere	irgendwo/nirgendwo
	eergentvoa/neergentvoa
everywhere	überall
	ueberall
far away/nearby	weit weg/inder Nähe
	vait vek/in dayr nayher
right/left	nach rechts/links
	nakh rekhts/links
to the right/left of	rechts/links von
	rekhts/links fon
straight ahead	geradeaus
	gerarder ows
via	über
	ueber
in	in
	in
on	auf
	owf
under	unter
	oonter
against	gegen
	gaygen
opposite	gegenüber
	gaygen ueber
next to	neben
	nayben
near	bei
	bai
in front of	vor
	for

in the centre	in der Mitte	
	in dayr mitter	
forward	nach vorn	
	nakh forn	
down	(nach) unten	
	(nakh) oonten	
up	(nach) oben	
	(nakh) owben	
inside	drinnen	
	drinnen	
outside	draussen/raus	
	drowssen/rows	
behind	(nach) hinten	
	(nakh) hinten	
at the front	vorn	
	forn	
at the back	hinten	
	hinten	
in the north	im Norden	
	im norden	
to the south	nach Süden	
	nakh zueden	
from the west	aus dem Westen	
	ows dem vesten	
from the east	aus dem Osten	
	ows daym ossten	
north, east, south, west of	nördlich/östlich/südlich/westlich von	
	noerdlikh/oestlikh/zuedlikh/vestlikh fon	

See also **5.4 Traffic signs**

Abfahrt/Ausgang
exit
Achtung
beware
Ankunft
arrival
Aufzug
lift
Auskunft
information
Bahnhof
station
Bitte nicht stören
Do not disturb
Drücken
push
Durchgang
throughway
Eingang
entrance
Eintritt frei/verboten
free entry/no entry
Empfang
reception
Erste Hilfe
first aid
Fahrkarten
tickets
Fahrstuhl
lift
Freibad
open-air swimming-
  pool

Fremdenverkehrs-
  verein
tourist information
Fussgänger
pedestrians
Gasthaus/Gasthof
inn
Gefahr
danger
Geöffnet
open
Gepäckannahme/
  -aufbewahrung
check-in/left-luggage
Geschlossen
closed
Gleis
platform
Kein Trinkwasser
No drinking water
Nicht berühren!
Please do not touch!
Notausgang/-treppe
emergency exit/stairs
Öffnungszeiten
opening hours
Pförtner
porter
Polizei
police
Rathaus
town hall/city hall

Rauchen verboten
no smoking
Reserviert
reserved
Rundfahrt
tour
Schliessfach
left luggage locker/
  safe deposit box
Schwimmbad
swimming-pool
Selbstbedienung
self-service
Stock
floor
Treppe
stairs
Vorsicht!
beware
Warnung
beware/warning
Warteraum/-saal
waiting room
Wechselstube
exchange office
Ziehen
pull
Zimmer frei/zu
  vermieten
vacancy (room)/room
  to let
Zugang
access/entry

1.8 Telephone alphabet

a	*ar*	wie Anton	*vee arnton*
ä	*ay*	wie Ärger	*vee airger*
b	*beh*	wie Berta	*vee berter*
c	*tseh*	wie Cäsar	*vee tsezer*
ch	*tseh-har*	wie Charlotte	*vee sharlotter*
d	*deh*	wie Dora	*vee doara*
e	*eh*	wie Emil	*vee aymil*
f	*ef*	wie Friedrich	*vee freedrikh*
g	*geh*	wie Gustav	*vee goostaf*
h	*hah*	wie Heinrich	*vee hainrikh*
i	*ee*	wie Ida	*vee eeda*
j	*yot*	wie Julius	*vee yoolius*
k	*kah*	wie Kaufmann	*vee kowfmann*
l	*el*	wie Ludwig	*vee loodvikh*
m	*em*	wie Martha	*vee marta*
n	*en*	wie Nordpol	*vee nortpole*
o	*oh*	wie Otto	*vee ottoa*
ö	*oe*	wie Ökonom	*vee oekonoam*
p	*peh*	wie Paula	*vee powla*
q	*koo*	wie Quelle	*vee kveller*
r	*air*	wie Richard	*vee rikhart*
sch	*es-tseh-har*	wie Schule	*vee shooler*
s	*es*	wie Samuel	*vee zarmooel*
t	*teh*	wie Theodor	*vee tayoador*
u	*oo*	wie Ulrich	*vee oolrikh*
ü	*ue*	wie Übermut	*vee uebermoot*
v	*fow*	wie Viktor	*vee viktor*
w	*veh*	wie Wilhelm	*vee vilhelm*
x	*iks*	wie Xanthippe	*vee ksantippeh*
y	*uepsilon*	wie Ypsilon	*vee uepsilon*
z	*tset*	wie Zacharias	*vee tsakharias*

1.9 Personal details

last/family name	(der) Nachname
	(dayr) nakhnarmer
first name(s)	(der) Vorname
	(dayr) fornarmer
initials	(der) Anfangsbuchstabe des Vornamens
	(dayr) an-fangs-bookh-shtarber dess fornarmenz
address (street/number)	(die) Anschrift (Strasse/Nummer)
	(dee) anshrift (shtrasser/noommer)
post code/town	(die) Postleitzahl/(der) Wohnort
	(dee) posst-lait-tsarl/(dayr) voanort
sex (male/female)	(das) Geschlecht (männlich/weiblich)
	(dass) geschlekht (maennlikh/vaiblikh)
nationality	(die) Staatsangehörigkeit
	(dee) shtarts-ange-hoerikh-kait
date of birth	(das) Geburtsdatum
	(dass) geboorts dartum
place of birth	(der) Geburtsort
	(dayr) geboorts ort
occupation	(der) Beruf
	(dayr) beroof
married/single/divorced	verheiratet/ledig/geschieden
	fairhai-rartet/laydikh/gescheeden
widowed	(die) Witwe/(der) Witwer
	(dee) vitveh/ (dayr) vitver
(number of) children	(Zahl der) Kinder
	(tsarl dayr) kinder
identity card/passport/ driving licence number	Personalausweis/Reisepass/ Führerschein- nummer
	pair zoanarl owsvaiz/raizerparss/ fuerershain nummer
place and date of issue	Ort und Datum der Ausstellung
	ort oont dartoom dayr owsshtelloong

2. Courtesies

● It is usual in Germany to shake hands on meeting and parting company.

2.1 Greetings

● The correct pronoun to use in formal greetings is *Sie* (zee) - which translates as 'you' – in the singular and plural. *Sie* should be employed when addressing people over the age of 18 except when talking to intimates. Conversation within the family, or between children, youths, students, friends and close work colleagues requires the use of the familiar second person pronoun *du* (doo). Please note that among adults it is usual for the older person to offer the more familiar address of *du* to the younger one.

Hello, Mr…	Guten Tag, Herr…
	gooten tark, hair...
Hello, Mrs…	Guten Tag, Frau…
	gooten tark, frow...
Hello, Peter.	Hallo, Peter.
	hallo, payter
Hi, Helen.	Tag, Helene.
	tark, helayner
Good morning.	Guten Morgen.
	gooten morgen
Good afternoon.	Guten Tag.
	gooten tark
Good evening.	Guten Abend.
	gooten arbent
How are you?	Wie geht's?
	vee gayts?
Fine, thank you, and you?	Sehr gut, und Ihnen?
	zayr goot, oont eenen?
Very well.	Ausgezeichnet.
	ows ge tsaikh net
Not very well.	Nicht besonders.
	nikht bezonderz

Not too bad.	Es geht.
	ez gayt
I'd better be going.	Dann geh' ich mal.
	dann gay' ikh mall
I have to be going.	Ich muss los. Ich werde erwartet.
Someone's waiting for me.	*ikh mooss loas. ikh verder ervartet*
Bye!	Tschüs!
	tshuess
Goodbye.	Auf Wiedersehen.
	owf veederzayn
See you soon.	Bis bald.
	biss balt
See you later.	Bis gleich.
	biss glaich
See you in a little while.	Bis dann.
	biss dann
Sleep well.	Schlafen Sie gut.
	shlarfen zee goot
Good night.	Gute Nacht.
	gooter nakht
All the best.	Alles Gute.
	alles gooter
Have fun.	Viel Vergnügen.
	feel fairgnuegen
Good luck.	Viel Glück.
	feel gluek
Have a nice holiday.	(Einen) schönen Urlaub.
	(ainen) shoenen oorlowp
Have a good trip.	Gute Reise.
	gooter raizer
Thank you, you too.	Danke, gleichfalls.
	danker, glaikhfalz
Say hello to...for me.	Schöne Grüsse an...
	shoener gruesser an...

2.2 How to ask a question

Who?	Wer?
	vayr?
Who's that?	Wer ist das?
	vayr ist dass?
What?	Was?
	vass?
What's there to see here?	Was gibt es hier zu sehen?
	vass gipt ez heer tsoo zayhen?
What kind of hotel is that?	Was für eine Art Hotel ist das?
	vass fuer ainer art hotel ist dass?
Where?	Wo?
	voe?
Where's the toilet?	Wo ist die Toilette?
	voe ist dee twaletter?
Where are you going?	Wohin gehen/(by car) fahren Sie?
	vohin gayhen/fahren zee?
Where are you from?	Woher kommen Sie?
	vohair kommen zee?
How?	Wie?
	vee?
How far is that?	Wie weit ist das?
	vee vait ist dass?
How long does that take?	Wie lange dauert das?
	vee langer dowert dass?
How long is the trip?	Wie lange dauert die Reise?
	vee langer dowert dee raizer?
How much?	Wieviel?
	veefeel?
How much is this?	Wieviel kostet das?
	veefeel kostet dass?
What time is it?	Wie spät ist es?
	vee shpayt ist ez?

Which?	Welcher (m), welches (n), welche (f, pl)
	velkher? velkherz? velkher?
Which glass is mine?	Welches Glas ist für mich?
	velkherz glars ist fuer mikh?
When?	Wann?
	vann?
When are you leaving?	Wann reisen Sie ab?
	vann raizen zee ap?
Why?	Warum?
	vahroom?
Could you help me, please?	Könnten Sie mir bitte helfen?
	koennten zee meer bitter helfen?
Could you point that out to me?	Können Sie mir das zeigen?
	koennen zee meer dass tsaygen?
Could you come with me, please?	Würden Sie bitte mit mir mitgehen?
	vuerden zee bitter mit meer mitgayhen?
Could you...?	Würden Sie bitte...?
	vuerden zee bitter...?
Could you reserve some tickets for me, please?	Würden Sie bitte Karten für mich reservieren?
	vuerden zee bitter karten fuer mikh rezerveeren?
Do you know...?	Wissen Sie...?
	vissen zee...?
Do you know another hotel, please?	Könnten Sie mir ein anderes Hotel empfehlen?
	koennten zee meer ain anderez hotel empfaylen?
Do you know whether...?	Wissen Sie ob..
	vissen zee op...
Do you have a...?	Haben Sie ein(en)/eine...?
	harben zee ain(en)/ainer...?
Do you have a vegetarian dish, please?	Haben Sie bitte ein vegetarisches Gericht?
	harben zee bitter ain vegetarishers gerikht?

I'd like...	Ich möchte gern ...
	ikh moekhter gayrn ...
I'd like a kilo of apples, please	Ich möchte bitte ein Kilo Äpfel
	ikh moekhter bitter ain kilo epfel
Can I...?	Darf ich...?
	darf ikh...?
Can I take this?	Darf ich dies mitnehmen?
	darf ikh dees mittnaymen?
Can I smoke here?	Darf ich hier rauchen?
	darf ikh heer rowkhen?
Could I ask you something?	Darf ich Sie etwas fragen?
	darf ikh zee etvass frargen?

2.3 How to reply

Yes, of course.	Ja, natürlich.
	yar, natuerlikh
No, I'm sorry.	Nein, es tut mir leid.
	Nain, ez toot meer lait
Yes, what can I do for you?	Ja, was kann ich für Sie tun?
	yar, vass kann ikh fuer zee toon?
Just a moment, please.	Einen Augenblick bitte.
	ainen owgen blick bitter
No, I don't have time now.	Nein, ich habe jetzt keine Zeit.
	nain, ikh haber yetst kainer tsait
No, that's impossible.	Nein, das ist unmöglich.
	nain, dass ist oonmoeglikh
I think so.	Ich glaube schon.
	ikh glowber shoan
I agree.	Ich glaube (es) auch.
	ikh glowber (ez) owkh
I hope so too.	Ich hoffe (es) auch.
	ikh hoffer (ez) owkh
No, not at all.	Nein, überhaupt nicht.
	nain, ueberhowpt nikht

No, no-one.	Nein, niemand.
	nain, neemant
No, nothing.	Nein, nichts.
	nain, nikhts
That's (not) right.	Das stimmt (nicht).
	dass shtimmt (nikht)
I (don't) agree.	Da stimme ich Ihnen (nicht) zu.
	dar shtimmer ikh eenen (nikht) tsoo
Okay.	Einverstanden.
	ain fair shtanden
Perhaps.	Vielleicht.
	feelaikht
I don't know.	Ich weiss es nicht.
	ikh vaiss es nikht

2.4 Thank you

Thank you.	Vielen Dank.
	feelen dunk
You're welcome.	Keine Ursache/gern geschehen.
	kainer oorzakher/gayrn geshayhen
Thank you very much.	Vielen herzlichen Dank.
	feelen hairtslikhen dunk
Very kind of you.	Sehr freundlich (von Ihnen).
	zayr froyntlikh (fon eenen)
I enjoyed it very much.	Es war mir ein Vergnügen.
	es var meer ain fairgnuegen
Thank you for your trouble.	Ich danke Ihnen für die Mühe.
	ikh dunker eenen fuer dee muer
You shouldn't have.	Das wäre nicht nötig gewesen.
	dass vayrer nikht noetikh gevayzen
That's all right.	Ist schon in Ordnung.
	ist shoan in ordnoong

2.5 Sorry

Excuse me.	Verzeihung.
	fair tsaioong
Sorry!	Entschuldigung!
	ent shool digoong
I'm sorry, I didn't know...	Entschuldigung, ich wusste nicht, dass...
	ent shool digung, ikh vuster nihkt dass...
I do apologise.	Ich bitte vielmals um Verzeihung.
	ikh bitter feelmarls oom fair tsaioong
Please don't hold it gainst me.	Nehmen Sie (es) mir bitte nicht übel.
	naymen zee (es) meer bitter nikht uebel
I'm sorry.	Es tut mir leid.
	ez toot meer lait
I didn't do it on purpose, it was an accident.	Ich habe es nicht mit Absicht getan, es war ein Versehen.
	ikh harber ez nikht mit apsikht getarn, ez var ain fairzayhen
That's all right.	Das macht nichts.
	dass makht nikhts
Never mind.	Lassen Sie nur.
	lassen zee noor
It could've happened to anyone.	Das kann jedem mal passieren.
	dass kann yaydem marl passeeren

2.6 Opinions

Which do you prefer?	Was ist Ihnen lieber?
	vass ist eenen leeber?
What do you think?	Was halten Sie davon?
	vass harlten zee dafonn?
I don't mind.	Es ist mir egal.
	ez ist meer egarl
Well done!	Sehr gut!
	zayr goot!
Not bad!	Nicht schlecht!
	nikht shlekht!
Great!	Ausgezeichnet!
	ows ge tsaykh net!
It's really nice here!	Hier ist es aber gemütlich!
	heer ist ez arber gemuetlikh!
How nice (for you)!	Wie hübsch/schön (für Sie/dich)!
	vee huepsh/shoen (fuer zee/dikh)!
I'm (not) very happy with...	Ich bin (nicht) sehr zufrieden über...
	ikh bin (nikht) zayr tsoofreeden ueber...
I'm glad...	Ich bin froh, dass...
	ikh bin froa, dass...
I'm having a great time.	Ich amüsiere mich sehr gut.
	ikh amuezeerer mikh zayr goot
I'm looking forward to it.	Ich freue mich drauf.
	ikh froyer mikh drowf
Impossible!	Unmöglich!
	oonmoeglikh!
That's terrible!	Wie scheußlich!
	vee shoysslikh!
What a pity!	Wie schade!
	vee sharder!
That's filthy!	Wie schmutzig/dreckig!
	vee shmootsikh/drekkikh!
What a load of rubbish!	(So'n) Quatsch!
	(zoan) kvatsh!

I don't like...	Ich mag kein/keine(n) (+ noun)/Ich (+ verb) nicht gern
	ikh mark kain/kainer(n)/ikh...nikht gayrn
I'm bored to death.	Ich langweile mich furchtbar.
	ikh langvailer mikh foorkhtbar
I've had enough.	Mir reicht's.
	meer raikhts
I was expecting something completely different.	Ich hatte etwas ganz anderes erwartet.
	ikh hatter etvass gants andererz airvartet

3. Conversation

3.1 I don't understand

I don't speak any/	Ich spreche kein/ein bisschen...
I speak a little...	*ikh shprekher kain/ain bisskhen...*
I'm English.	Ich bin Engländer/in.
	ikh bin englender (m)/englenderi (f)
I'm Scottish.	Ich bin Schotte/Schottin.
	ikh bin shotter/shottin
I'm Irish.	Ich bin Irländer/Irländerin.
	ikh bin earlender/earlenderin
I'm Welsh.	Ich bin Waliser/Waliserin.
	ikh bin valeezer/valeezerin
Do you speak English/	Sprechen Sie Englisch/Französisch/
French/ German?	Deutsch?
	shprekhen zee english/frantsoezish/
	doytsh?
Is there anyone who speaks...?	Ist hier jemand, der...spricht?
	ist heer yaymant, dayr ... shprikht?
I beg your pardon?	Wie bitte?
	vee bitter?
I (don't) understand.	Ich verstehe (es) (nicht).
	ikh fair shtayher (es) (nikht)
Do you understand me?	Verstehen Sie mich?
	fair shtayhen zee mikh?
Could you repeat that, please?	Würden Sie das bitte wiederholen?
	vuerden zee dass bitter vee-der-hoalen?
Could you speak more	Könnten Sie etwas langsamer sprechen?
slowly, please?	*koennten zee etvass langzarmer*
	shprekhen?
What does that word mean?	Was bedeutet das/dieses Wort?
	vass bedoytet dass/deezez vort?
Is that similar to/	Ist das (ungefähr) dasselbe wie...?
the same as...?	*ist das (oongefair) dass zelber vee...?*
Could you write that down	Könnten Sie mir das bitte aufschreiben?
for me, please?	*koennten zee meer dass bitter*
	owfshraiben?

Could you spell that for me, please?

Könnten Sie mir das bitte buchstabieren?

koennten zee meer dass bitter bookhshtabeeren?

(See **1.8 Telephone alphabet**)

Could you point that out in this phrase book, please?

Könnten Sie mir das in diesem Sprachführer zeigen?

koennten zee meer dass in deezem shprakhfuerer tsaigen?

One moment, please, I have to look it up.

Augenblick bitte, ich muß es erst suchen.

owgenblick bitte, ikh mooss ez erst zookhen

I can't find the word/ the sentence.

Ich kann das Wort/den Satz nicht finden.

ikh kann dass vort/dayn zats nikht finden

How do you say that in...?

Wie sagt man das auf...?

vee zarkt mann dass owf...

How do you pronounce that?

Wie spricht man das aus?

vee shprikht mann dass ows?

3.2 Introductions

My name's...

Ich heisse...

ikh haisser...

I'm...

Ich bin...

ikh bin...

What's your name?

Wie heissen Sie?

vee haissen zee?

May I introduce...?

Darf ich Ihnen vorstellen...?

darf ikh eenen forshtellen...?

This is my wife/daughter/ mother/girlfriend.

Dies ist meine Frau/Tochter/Mutter/ Freundin.

deez ist mainer frow/tokhter/mootter/ froyndin

– my husband/son/ father/boyfriend.

Dies ist mein Mann/Sohn/Vater/Freund.

dees ist main mann/zoan/farter/froynt

How do you do.	Guten Tag/Abend, nett Sie kennenzulernen.
	gooten tark/arbent, nett zee kennen tsoo layrnen
Pleased to meet you.	Angenehm.
	angenaym
Where are you from?	Woher kommen Sie?
	voahair kommen zee?
I'm from England/Scotland/ Ireland/Wales.	Ich komme aus England/Schottland/ Irland/Wales.
	ikh kommer ows englant/shottlant/ earlant/vaylz
What city do you live in?	In welcher Stadt wohnen Sie?
	in velkher shtatt voanen zee?
In..., it's near...	In...., das ist in der Nähe von...
	in...., dass ist in dayr nayher fon...
Have you been here long?	Sind Sie schon lange hier?
	zint zee shoan langer heer?
A few days.	Ein paar Tage.
	ain pahr targer
How long are you staying here?	Wie lange bleiben Sie hier?
	vee langer blaiben zee heer?
We're (probably) leaving tomorrow/in two weeks.	Wir reisen (wahrscheinlich) morgen/in zwei Wochen ab.
	veer raizen (varshainlikh) morgun/in tsvai vokhen ap
Where are you staying?	Wo wohnen Sie?
	vo voanen zee?
In a hotel/an apartment.	In einem Hotel/Appartement.
	in ainem hotel/apartament
On a camp site.	Auf einem Campingplatz.
	owf ainem camping plats
With friends/relatives.	Bei Freunden/Verwandten.
	bai froynden/fairvanten
Are you here on your own/ with your family?	Sind Sie hier allein/mit Ihrer Familie?
	zint zee heer allain/mit eerer fameelyeh?

I'm on my own.	Ich bin allein.
	ikh bin allain
I'm with my partner/ wife/husband.	Ich bin hier mit meinem Partner/meiner Partnerin/meiner Frau/meinem Mann.
	ikh bin heer mit mainem partner/mainer partnerin/mainer frow/mainem man
– with my family.	Ich bin hier mit meiner Familie.
	ikh bin hier mit mainer fameelyeh
– with relatives.	Ich bin hier mit Verwandten.
	ikh bin hier mit fairvanten
– with a friend/friends.	Ich bin hier mit einem Freund/einer Freundin/Freunden.
	ikh bin hier mit ainem froynt/ainer froyndin/froynden
Are you married?	Sind Sie verheiratet?
	zint zee fairhairartet?
Do you have a steady boyfriend/girlfriend?	Hast du eine feste Freundin (f)/einen festen Freund (m)?
	hast doo ainer fester froyndin/aynen festen froynt?
That's none of your business.	Das geht Sie nichts an.
	dass gayt zee nikhts an
I'm married.	Ich bin verheiratet.
	ikh bin fairhai rartet
– single.	Ich bin Junggeselle/Junggesellin.
	ikh bin yoong ge zeller/yoong ge zellin
– separated.	Ich lebe getrennt.
	ikh layber getrennt
– divorced.	Ich bin geschieden.
	ikh bin gesheeden
– a widow/widower.	Ich bin Witwe/Witwer.
	ikh bin vitveh/vitver
I live alone/with someone.	Ich lebe allein/mit jemandem zusammen.
	ikh layber allain/mit yaymandem tsoozammen

Do you have any children/ grandchildren?	Haben Sie Kinder/Enkel?
	harben zee kinder/enkell?
How old are you?	Wie alt sind Sie?
	vee alt zint zee?
How old is he/she?	Wie alt ist er/sie?
	vee alt ist ayr/zee?
I'm...years old.	Ich bin...Jahre alt.
	ikh bin...yahrer alt
He's/she's...years old.	Sie/er ist...Jahre alt.
	zee/ayr ist...yahrer alt
What do you do for a living?	Was für eine Arbeit machen Sie?
	vass fuer ainer arbait makhen zee?
I work in an office.	Ich arbeite in einem Büro.
	ikh arbaiter in ainem buero
I'm a student/I'm at school.	Ich studiere/gehe zur Schule.
	ikh shtoodearer/gayher tsoor shooler
I'm unemployed.	Ich bin arbeitslos.
	ikh bin arbaitsloaz
I'm retired.	Ich bin pensioniert/Rentner/Rentnerin.
	ikh bin pen zeeoa neert/rentner/rentnerin
I have taken early retirement.	Ich bin im Vorruhestand.
	ikh bin im for-rooher-shtant
Do you like your job?	Macht Ihnen die Arbeit Spass?
	makht eenen dee arbait shpass?
Most of the time.	Mal ja, mal nein.
	marl yar, marl nain
I usually do, but I prefer holidays.	Meistens schon, aber Urlaub ist schöner.
	maistens shoan, arber oorlowp ist shoener

3.3 Starting/ending a conversation

Could I ask you something?	Dürfte ich Sie etwas fragen?
	duerfter ikh zee etvass frargen?
Excuse me.	Entschuldigen Sie bitte.
	ent shool digen zee bitter
Excuse me, could you help me?	Entschuldigung, könnten Sie mir helfen?
	ent shool digoong, koennten zee meer helfen?
Yes, what's the problem?	Ja, was ist denn los?
	yar, vass ist den loas?
What can I do for you?	Was kann ich für Sie tun?
	vass kan ikh fuer zee toon?
Sorry, I don't have time now.	Bedaure, ich habe jetzt keine Zeit.
	bedowrer, ikh harber yetst kainer tsayt
Do you have a light?	Haben Sie Feuer?
	harben zee foyerr?
May I join you?	Darf ich mich zu Ihnen setzen?
	darf ikh mikh tsoo eenen zetsen?
Could you take a picture of me/us?	Würden Sie ein Foto von mir/uns machen?
	vuerden zee ain foto fon meer/oons makhen?
Leave me alone.	Lassen Sie mich in Ruhe.
	lassen zee mikh in rooher
Get lost.	Machen Sie, daß Sie wegkommen.
	makhen zee dass zee vek kommen

3.4 Congratulations and condolences

Happy birthday/ many happy returns.	Meinen Glückwunsch zum Geburtstag.
	mainen gluekvoonsh tsoom geboortstark
Please accept my condolences.	Mein Beileid.
	main bailait
I'm very sorry for you.	Es tut mir ja so leid für Sie.
	ez toot meer yar zo lait fuer zee

3.5 A chat about the weather

See also **1.5 The weather**

It's so hot/cold today!	Heute ist es aber warm/kalt!
	hoyter ist ez arber varm/kalt!
Nice weather, isn't it?	Angenehmes Wetter, nicht?
	angenaymers vetter, nikht?
What a wind/storm!	So ein Wind/Sturm!
	zo ain vint/shtoorm
All that rain/snow!	Wie das regnet/schneit!
	vee dass raygnet/shnait!
All that fog!	Das ist vielleicht ein Nebel!
	dass ist feelaikht ain naybel!
Has the weather been like this for long here?	Ist das Wetter hier schon lange so?
	ist dass vetter heer shoan langer zo?
Is it always this hot/cold here?	Ist es hier immer so warm/kalt?
	ist es heer immer zo varm/kalt?
Is it always this dry/wet here?	Ist es hier immer so trocken/nass?
	ist es heer immer zo trokken/nass?
What will the weather be like tomorrow?	Wie wird das Wetter morgen?
	vee virt dars vetter moargen?

3.6 Hobbies

Do you have any hobbies?	Haben Sie Hobbys?
	harben zee hobbies?
I like painting/reading/ photography/DIY.	Ich stricke/lese/fotografiere/ zeichne gern.
	ikh shtrikker/layzer/fotograffearer/ tsaikhner gayrn
I like music.	Ich liebe Musik.
	ikh leeber moozeek
I like playing the guitar/piano.	Ich spiele gern Gitarre/Klavier.
	ikh shpeeler gayrn gitarrer/klaveer

I like going to the movies.	Ich gehe gern ins Kino.
	ikh gayher gayrn ins keeno
I like travelling/sport/ fishing/walking.	Ich reise/angle/wandre gern.
	ikh raizer/angler/vanderer gayrn

3.7 Being the host(ess)

See also **4 Eating out**

Can I offer you a drink?	Darf ich Ihnen etwas zu trinken anbieten?
	darf ikh eenen etvass tsoo trinken anbeeten?
What would you like to drink?	Was möchtest du trinken?
	vass moekhtest doo trinken?
Something non-alcoholic, please.	Gern etwas ohne Alkohol.
	gayrn etvass oaner alkohol
Would you like a cigarette/ cigar?	Möchten Sie eine Zigarette/Zigarre?
	moekhten zee ainer tsigarretter/ tsigarrer?
I don't smoke.	Ich rauche nicht.
	ikh rowkher nikht

3.8 Invitations

Are you doing anything tonight?	Hast du heute abend was vor?
	hast doo hoyter arbent vass for?
Do you have any plans for today/this afternoon/ tonight?	Haben Sie schon Pläne für heute/heute nachmittag/heute abend?
	harben zee shoan playner fuer hoyter/ hoyter nakhmittark/hoyter arbent?
Would you like to go out with me?	Haben Sie Lust, mit mir auszugehen?
	harben zee loost, mit meer ows tsoo gayhen?

Would you like to go dancing with me?	Haben Sie Lust, mit mir tanzen zu gehen?
	harben zee loost, mitt meer tantsen tsoo gayhen?
Would you like to have lunch/ dinner with me?	Haben Sie Lust, mit mir zu essen?
	harben zee loost, mit meer tsoo essen?
Would you like to come to the beach with me?	Haben Sie Lust, an den Strand zu gehen?
	harben zee loost, an den shtrant tsoo gayhen?
Would you like to come into town with us?	Haben Sie Lust, mit uns in die Stadt zu gehen/fahren?
	harben zee loost, mit oons in dee shtatt tsoo gayhen/fahren?
Would you like to come and see some friends with us?	Haben Sie Lust, mit uns zu Freunden zu gehen?
	harben zee loost, mit oons tsoo froynden tsoo gayhen?
Shall we dance?	Wollen wir tanzen?
	vollen veer tantsen?
– sit at the bar?	Kommst du mit an die Bar?
	kommst doo mit an dee bar?
– get something to drink?	Wollen wir etwas trinken?
	vollen veer etvass trinken?
– go for a walk/drive?	Wollen wir ein bisschen spazierengehen/ Auto fahren?
	vollen veer ain bisskhen shpatseeren gayhen/owto fahren?
Yes, all right.	Ja, gut.
	yar, goot
Good idea.	Gute Idee.
	gooter eeday
No (thank you).	Nein (danke).
	nain (dunker)
Maybe later.	Vielleicht später.
	feelaikht shpayter

I don't feel like it.	Dazu habe ich keine Lust.
	datsoo harber ikh kainer loost
I don't have time	Ich habe keine Zeit.
	ikh harber kainer tsait
I already have a date	Ich habe schon eine Verabredung.
	ikh harber shoan ainer fair ap ray doong
I'm not very good at dancing/ volleyball/swimming	Ich kann nicht tanzen/Volleyball spielen/ schwimmen.
	ikh kann nikht tantsen/volleyball shpeelen/shvimmen

3.9 Paying a compliment

You look wonderful!	Sie sehen (ja) fabelhaft aus!
	zee zayhen (yar) farbelhaft ows!
I like your car!	Schönes/tolles Auto!
	shoenez/tollez owto!
I like your ski outfit!	Hübscher Skianzug!
	huepsher shee antsook!
You're a nice boy/girl.	Du bist lieb.
	doo bist leep
What a sweet child!	Was für ein liebes Kind!
	vass fuer ain leebes kint!
You're a wonderful dancer!	Sie tanzen sehr gut!
	zee tantsen zayr goot!
You're a wonderful cook!	Sie kochen sehr gut!
	zee kokhen zayr goot!
You're a terrific football player!	Sie spielen sehr gut Fussball!
	zee shpeelen zayr goot foossball!

3.10 Romance and relationships

I like being with you. Ich bin gern mit dir zusammen.
ikh bin gayrn mit deer tsoozammen

I've missed you so much. Ich habe dich so vermisst.
ikh haber dikh zo fairmisst

I dreamed about you. Ich habe von dir geträumt.
ikh haber fon deer getroymt

I think about you all day Ich muss den ganzen Tag an dich denken
ikh muss den gantsen tark an dikh denken

You have such a sweet smile. Du lächelst so süss.
doo laekhelst zo suess

You have such beautiful eyes. Du hast so schöne Augen.
doo hast zo shoener owgen

I'm in love with you. Ich habe mich in dich verliebt.
ikh haber mikh in dikh fairleept

I'm in love with you too. Ich mich auch in dich.
ikh mikh owkh in dikh

I love you. Ich liebe dich.
ikh leeber dikh

I love you too. Ich dich auch.
ikh dikh owkh

I don't feel as strongly about you. Ich empfinde nicht dasselbe für dich.
ikh empfinder nikht dass selber fuer dikh

I already have a boyfriend/girlfriend. Ich habe schon einen Freund/ein Freundin.
ikh harber shoan ainen froynt/ainer froyndin

I'm not ready for that. Ich bin noch nicht so weit.
ikh bin nokh nikht zo vait

This is going too fast for me. Es geht mir viel zu schnell.
ez gayt meer feel tsoo shnell

Take your hands off me. Rühr mich nicht an.
ruehr mikh nikht an

Okay, no problem. O.K., kein Problem.
oakay, kain problaym

Will you stay with me tonight?	Bleibst du heute nacht bei mir?
	blaipst doo hoyter nakht bai meer?
I'd like to go to bed with you.	Ich möchte mit dir schlafen.
	ikh moekhter mit deer shlarfen
Only if we use a condom.	Nur mit Präservativ/Kondom.
	noor mitt prezervatif/kondoam
We have to be careful about STDs.	Wir müssen vorsichtig sein wegen STDs.
	veer muessen forsikhtikh zain vaygen es te de
That's what they all say.	Das sagen alle.
	dass zargen aller
We shouldn't take any risks.	Wir wollen lieber kein Risiko eingehen.
	veer vollen leeber kain reeziko aingayhen
Do you have a condom?	Hast du ein Präservativ/Kondom?
	hast doo ain prezervatif/kondoam?
No? In that case we won't do it.	Nein? Dann machen wir's nicht.
	nain? dann makhen veer's nikht

3.11 Arrangements

When will I see you again?	Wann sehe ich Sie/dich wieder?
	vann zayher ikh zee/dikh veeder?
Are you free over the weekend?	Haben Sie am Wochenende Zeit?
	harben zee am vokhenender tsait?
What shall we arrange?	Wie verbleiben wir?
	vee fairblaiben veer?
Where shall we meet?	Wo wollen wir uns treffen?
	voa vollen veer oons treffen?
Will you pick me/us up?	Holen Sie mich/uns ab?
	hoalen zee mikh/oons ap?
Shall I pick you up?	Soll ich Sie abholen?
	zoll ikh zee apholen?
I have to be home by...	Ich muss um...Uhr zu Hause sein.
	ikh muss oom...ooer tsoo howzer zain

3.12 Saying goodbye

I don't want to see you anymore.	Ich will Sie nicht mehr sehen.	
	ikh vill zee nikht mayr zayhen	
Can I take you home?	Darf ich Sie nach Hause bringen?	
	darf ikh zee nakh howzer bringen?	
Can I write/call you?	Darf ich Ihnen schreiben/Sie anrufen?	
	darf ikh eenen shraiben/zee anroofen?	
Will you write/call me?	Schreiben Sie mir/rufen Sie mich an?	
	shraiben zee meer/roofen zee mikh an?	
Can I have your address/ phone number?	Geben Sie mir Ihre Adresse/ Telefonnummer?	
	gayben zee meer eerer adresser/telefoan noomer?	
Thanks for everything.	Vielen Dank für alles.	
	feelen dunk fuer alless	
It was very nice.	Es war sehr schön	
	es var zayr shoen	
Say hello to...	Grüssen Sie...	*gruessen zee...*
All the best.	Alles Gute.	*alles gooter*
Good luck.	Viel Erfolg weiter.	*feel erfolk vaiter*
When will you be back?	Wann kommst du wieder?	
	vann kommst doo veeder?	
I'll be waiting for you.	Ich warte auf dich.	
	ikh varter owf dikh	
I'd like to see you again.	Ich möchte dich gern wiedersehen.	
	ikh moekhter dikh gayrn veeder zayhen	
I hope we meet again soon.	Ich hoffe, wir sehen uns wieder.	
	ikh hoffer, veer zayhen oons veeder	
Here is our address. If you're ever in the UK...	Dies ist unsere Adresse. Wenn Sie je in England sind...	
	deez ist oonzerer adresser - venn zee yay in englant zint...	
You'd be more than welcome.	Sie sind uns herzlich willkommen.	
	zee zint oons hertslikh villkommen	

4. Eating out

● In Germany people usually have three main meals:

1 *Frühstück* (breakfast) between approx. 6.30 and 10am. Breakfast is varied and can consist of coffee or herbal infusions, cereal (particularly muesli), bread rolls or slices of *Vollkornbrot* (whole-wheat bread) with a choice of butter, jam, ham or cheese. On Sundays this array is often complemented by boiled eggs.

2 *Mittagessen* (lunch) approximately between midday and 2pm. Traditionally lunch consists of a hot dish and is the most important meal of the day. Offices and shops often close while lunch is taken at home, in a restaurant or canteen. It usually consists of two or three courses:
– starter
– main course
– dessert

3 *Abendessen* (dinner)/*Vesper* (cold evening meal in southern Germany) between 6 and 9.30pm. This either consists of a light hot meal or a cold meal such as slices of bread with cold meat, cheese and salad.

At about 3.30pm, particularly on a Sunday, coffee and all kinds of cakes and pastries are taken.

4.1 On arrival

I'd like to book a table for seven o'clock, please.	Kann ich einen Tisch für sieben Uhr reservieren lassen?
	kann ikh ainen tish fuer zeeben ooer rezerveeren lassen?
I'd like a table for two, please.	Bitte einen Tisch für zwei Personen.
	bitter ainen tish fuer tsvai perzoanen
We've/we haven't booked.	Wir haben (nicht) reserviert.
	veer harben (nikht) rezerveert
Is the restaurant open yet?	Hat die Küche schon geöffnet?
	hat dee kuekher shoan geoeffnet?
What time does the restaurant open/close?	Wann öffnet/schliesst die Küche?
	vann oeffnet/shleest dee kuekher?
Can we wait for a table?	Können wir auf einen Tisch warten?
	koennen veer owf ainen tish varten?

Haben Sie reserviert?	Do you have a reservation?
Unter welchem Namen?	What name, please?
Hierher bitte.	This way, please.
Dieser Tisch ist reserviert.	This table is reserved
In einer Viertelstunde wird ein Tisch frei.	We'll have a table free in fifteen minutes.
Möchten Sie solange (an der Bar) warten?	Would you like to wait (at the bar)?

Do we have to wait long?

Müssen wir lange warten?
muessen veer langer varten?

Is this seat taken?

Ist dieser Platz frei?
ist deezer plats frai?

Could we sit here/there?

Können wir uns hierher/dahin setzen?
koennen veer oons heerhair/darhin zetsen?

Can we sit by the window?

Können wir uns ans Fenster setzen?
koennen veer oons ans fenster zetsen?

Can we eat outside?

Können wir auch draussen essen?
koennen veer owkh drowsen essen?

Do you have another chair for us?

Könnten Sie uns noch einen Stuhl bringen?
koennten zee oons nokh ainen shtool bringen?

Do you have a highchair?

Könnten Sie uns einen Kinderstuhl bringen?
koennten zee oons ainen kindershtool bringen?

Could you warm up this bottle/jar for me?

Könnten Sie mir dieses Fläschchen/ Gläschen aufwärmen?
koennten zee meer deezez fleshkhen/ glayzkhen owfvermen?

Not too hot, please.

Nicht zu heiss bitte.
nikht tsoo haiss bitter

Is there somewhere I can
change the baby's nappy?

Gibt es hier einen Raum, wo ich das
Baby wickeln kann?
*gipt ez heer ainen rowm vo ikh dass
bayby vikkeln kann?*

Where are the toilets?

Wo ist die Toilette?
vo ist dee twaletter?

4.2 Ordering

Waiter!

Herr Ober!
herr oaber!

Waitress!

Bedienung!
bedeenoong!

Sir!

Bitte!
bitter!

We'd like something to
eat/a drink.

Wir möchten gern etwas essen/trinken.
*veer moekhten gayrn etvass essen/
trinken*

Could I have a quick meal?

Könnte ich schnell etwas essen?
koennter ikh shnell etvass essen?

We don't have much time.

Wir haben wenig Zeit.
veer harben vaynikh tsait

We'd like to have a drink first.

Wir möchten erst noch etwas trinken.
veer moekhten ayrst nokh etvass trinken

Could we see the
menu/wine list, please?

Wir hätten gern die Speisekarte/
Weinkarte/(Getränkekarte).
*veer hetten gayrn dee spaizer karter/vain
karter (gertrenker karte)*

Could I have a cup of
tea/coffee/hot chocolate,
please?

Könnte ich bitte eine Tasse
Tee/Kaffee/heiße Schokolade haben?
*Koennter ish bitter ainer tasser tay/
kafey/ haisser shoakoalarder harben?*

Could I have a glass of water/
fresh orange juice/cola,
please?

Könnte ich bitte ein Glas Wasser/
frischen Orangensaft/Cola haben?
*Koennter ish bitter ain glars vasser/
frishen oarongensuft/koalar harben?*

Do you have a menu in English?	Haben Sie eine Speisekarte in Englisch?
	harben zee ainer shpayzer karter in english?
Do you have a dish of the day?	Haben Sie ein Tagesmenü/Touristenmenü?
	harben zee ain targes menyoo/toorissten menyoo?
We haven't made a choice yet.	Wir haben noch nicht gewählt.
	veer harben nokh nikht gevaylt
What do you recommend?	Was können Sie uns empfehlen?
	vass koennen zee oons empfaylen?
What are the specialities of the region/the house?	Welches sind die Spezialitäten dieser Gegend/des Hauses?
	velkhes zint dee shpetseeali tayten deezer gegent/dez howzez?
I like strawberries/olives.	Ich liebe Erdbeeren/Oliven.
	ikh leeber ertbeeren/olleeven
I don't like meat/fish.	Ich mag kein Fleisch/keinen Fisch.
	ikh mark kain flaish/kainen fish
What's this?	Was ist das?
	vass ist dass?
Does it have...in it?	Ist das mit...?
	ist dass mit...?
What does it taste like?	Womit kann man das vergleichen?
	vo-mitt kann mann dass fairglaikhen?

Möchten Sie essen/speisen?	Would you like to eat?
Haben Sie schon gewählt?	Have you decided?
Möchten Sie eine Nachspeise?	Would you like a dessert?
Was darf es sein?	What would you like?
Guten Appetit!	Enjoy your meal!
Darf/Dürfte ich jetzt abrechnen?	May I ask you to settle the bill, please?

Is this a hot or a cold dish?	Ist dieses Gericht warm oder kalt?
	ist deezes gerikht varm oader kalt?
Is this sweet?	Ist es eine Süßspeise?
	ist ez ainer suess shpaizer?
Is this spicy?	Ist es pikant/scharf?
	ist es peekant/sharf?
Do you have anything else, please?	Haben Sie vielleicht etwas anderes?
	harben zee feelaihkt etvass anderez?
I'm on a salt-free diet.	Ich darf kein Salz essen.
	ikh darf kain zalts essen
I can't eat pork.	Ich darf kein Schweinefleisch essen.
	ikh darf kain shvainer flaish essen
– sugar.	Ich darf keinen Zucker essen.
	ikh darf kainen tsooker essen
– fatty foods.	Ich darf kein Fett essen.
	ikh darf kain fet essen
– (hot) spices.	Ich darf keine scharfen Gewürze essen.
	ikh darf kainer sharfen gewuertser essen
Is this food kosher/halal?	Ist dieses Essen koscher/halal?
	ist deezes essen kosher/harlarl?
Does this food contain nuts?	Sind in diesem Essen Nüsse enthalten?
	zind in deezem essen nuesse enthulten?
I have an allergy to nuts/ seafood/wheat.	Ich bin allergisch gegen Nüsse/ Meeresfrüchte/Weizen.
	ish bin arlergish gegen nuesse/ mayresfrueshte/waitsen.
I'll have what those people are having.	Ich möchte/wir möchten gern dasselbe wie die Leute da.
	ikh moekhter/veer moekhten gayrn dass selber vee dee loyter dar
I'd like...	Ich möchte...
	ikh moekhter...
We're not having a starter.	Wir nehmen keine Vorspeise.
	veer naymen kainer for shpaizer

The child will share what we're having.	Das Kind isst etwas von unserem Menü mit.	
	dass kint ist etvass fon oonzerem menyoo mit	
Could I have some more bread, please?	Noch etwas Brot bitte.	
	nokh etvass broat bitter	
– a bottle of water/wine.	Noch eine Flasche (Mineral)wasser/ Wein bitte.	
	nokh ainer flasher (minerarl)vasser/ vain bitter	
– another helping of...	Noch eine Portion....bitte.	
	nokh ainer portseeoan...bitter	
– some salt and pepper.	Würden Sie bitte Salz und Pfeffer bringen?	
	vuerden zee bitter zalts unt pfeffer bringen?	
– a napkin.	Würden Sie bitte eine Serviette bringen?	
	vuerden zee bitter ainer zerviyetter bringen?	
– a spoon.	Würden Sie bitte einen Löffel bringen?	
	vuerden zee bitter ainen loeffel bringen?	
– a glass of water.	Würden Sie bitte ein Glas Wasser bringen?	
	vuerden zee bitter ain glars vasser bringen?	
– a straw (for the child).	Würden Sie bitte (für das Kind) einen Trinkhalm bringen?	
	vuerden zee bitter (fuer dass kint) ainen trinkhalm bringen?	
Enjoy your meal!	Guten Appetit!	
	gooten appeteet!	
You too!	Danke, gleichfalls!	
	dunker, glaikhfals!	
Cheers!	Prost/zum Wohl!	
	prrosst/tsoom voal!	
The next round's on me.	Die nächste Runde gebe ich (aus).	
	dee nexter roonder gayber ikh (ows)	

Could we have a doggy bag, please?	Dürfen wir die Reste mitnehmen?
	duerfen veer dee rester mitnaymen?

4.3 The bill

See also **8.2 Settling the bill**

How much is this dish?	Wieviel kostet dieses Gericht?
	veefeel kostet deezes gerikht?
Could I have the bill, please?	Die Rechnung bitte.
	dee rekhnoong bitter
All together.	Alles zusammen.
	alles tsoozammen
Everyone pays separately.	Getrennt zahlen.
	getrennt tsarlen
Could we have the menu again, please?	Dürften wir die Karte noch mal sehen?
	duerften veer dee karter nokh marl zayhen?
The...is not on the bill.	Der/die/das...steht nicht auf der Rechnung.
	der/dee/dass...shtayt nihkt owf dayr rekhnoong

4.4 Complaints

It's taking a very long time.	Das dauert aber lange.
	dass dowert arber langer
We've been here an hour already.	Wir sitzen hier schon seit einer Stunde.
	veer zitsen heer shoan zait ainer shtoonder
This must be a mistake.	Das muss ein Irrtum sein.
	dass muss ain eartoom zain
This is not what I ordered.	Das habe ich nicht bestellt.
	dass harber ikh nikht beshtellt

I ordered...	Ich habe um...gebeten.
	ikh harber oom...gebayten.
There's a dish missing.	Es fehlt ein Gericht.
	ez faylt ain gerikht
This is broken/not clean.	Das ist kaputt/nicht sauber.
	dass ist kapoott/nikht zowber
The food's cold.	Das Essen ist kalt.
	dass essen ist kalt
– not fresh.	Das Essen ist nicht frisch.
	dass essen ist nikht frish
– too salty/sweet/spicy.	Das Essen ist versalzen/zu süss/scharf.
	dass essen ist fairzaltsen/tsoo zuess/sharf
The meat's not done.	Das Fleisch ist nicht gar.
	dass flaish ist nikht garr
– overdone.	Das Fleisch ist zu sehr durchgebraten.
	dass flaish ist tsoo zayr doorkh gebrarten
– tough.	Das Fleisch ist zäh.
	dass flaish ist tsay
– off.	Das Fleisch ist verdorben.
	dass flaish ist fairdorben
Could I have something else instead of this?	Können Sie mir hierfür etwas anderes bringen?
	koennen zee meer heerfuerr etvass anderez bringen?
The bill/this amount is not right.	Die Rechnung/dieser Betrag stimmt nicht.
	dee rekhnoong/deezer betrark shtimmt nikht
We didn't have this.	Das haben wir nicht gehabt.
	dass harben veer nikht gehapt
There's no paper in the toilet.	Auf der Toilette ist kein Toilettenpapier.
	owf der twaletter ist kain twaletten-papeer
Will you call the manager, please?	Würden Sie bitte den Chef rufen?
	vuerden zee bitter den shef roofen?

4.5 Paying a compliment

That was a wonderful meal.

Wir haben herrlich gegessen.
veer harben hairlikh gegessen

The food was excellent.

Es hat uns ausgezeichnet geschmeckt.
ez hat oons owsge tsaikhnet geshmekt

The...in particular was

Vor allem der/die/das...war
hervorragend.

delicious.

*for allem dayr/dee/dass...var
hair-for-rargent*

4.6 The menu

Bedienung
einschliesslich
service included
Beilagen
side-dishes
Erfrischungsgetränke
refreshment drinks
Fisch
fish
Frühstück
breakfast
Gebäck
biscuits, pastries,
buns, tarts, tartlets
Gedeck
set meal/place
Gerichte
dishes

Getränke (karte)
beverages/list of
beverages (café) or
wine list (restaurant)
Happen
snack
Hauptgerichte
main courses
Köstlichkeiten
delicacies
Kuchen
cake(s)
Meeresfrüchte
seafood
Nachspeisen
desserts
Spezialitäten
specialities

Suppen
soups
Tagesmenü
menu of the day
Tagesteller
dish of the day
Torten
gateau/flan (with
fruit)
Vorspeisen
starters
Weine
wines
Weinkarte
wine list
Zwischengerichte
entrée/snack

Aal
eel

Apfel
apple

Äpfel im Schlafrock
baked apples in puff
pastry

Apfelsine
orange

Aspik
aspic

Aufschnitt
sliced cold meat or
(rarer) cheese

Austern
oysters

Bauern-
farmer's/rustic

-brot
coarse rye bread

-frühstück
bacon and potato
omelette

Beeren
berries

Birne
pears

Bismarckhering
Bismarck herring
(filleted pickled
herring)

Blaubeere
blueberry

Blaukraut
red cabbage

**Bohnen (grüne,
grosse)**
green beans

Braten
roast

Bratkartoffeln
fried potatoes

Brause
pop/lemonade

Bries(chen), Briesel
dish containing
sweetbreads
of animals (mostly
calves)

Brombeere
blackberry

Brot
bread

Brötchen
bread rolls

Brühe
clear soup/stock

Brust
breast

Bündner Fleisch
smoked ham from
the region of
Graubünden in
Switzerland

Butt
flounder/butt

Butter
butter

Chicoree
chicory

Curry
curry

Dampfnudeln
sweet yeast dumpling
cooked in milk and
sugar

Dattel
date

Dörr-
dried

Dorsch
cod

Eierkuchen (dünn)
(thin) pancakes

Eierstich
egg based ingredient
of some soups

Eintopf
stew

Eisbecher
sundae(s)

Eisbombe
ice cream cake

Endivie
endive

Ente
duck

Erbsen
peas

Erdbeere
strawberry

Essig
vinegar

Fadennudeln
vermicelli

Feige
fig

Filetsteak
fillet steak

Fisch
fish

Fisolen
green beans

Fleisch
meat

Flusskrebs
crayfish

Frikassee (Hühner-)
(chicken) fricassee

Frittatensuppe
soup containing strips
of pancake

Frühlingsrolle
spring rolls

Gänseleber
goose liver

Garnele
shrimp

gebraten
fried

gedünstet
braised

Geflügel
poultry

gefüllt
filled/stuffed

gekocht
boiled

Gelee
jelly

Gemüse
vegetables

geräuchert
smoked

Geschnetzeltes
meat cut into strips,
stewed to produce
a thick sauce

Geselchtes
salted and smoked
meat

gespickt
larded/fried meat with
strips of bacon

getrocknet
dried

gewürzt
seasoned

Glühwein
mulled wine

Grog
grog

Gulasch
goulash

Gurke (saure-)
(pickled) gherkins

Hähnchen/Hühnchen
chicken

Hase
hare

Haselnuss
hazelnut

Hasenpfeffer
jugged hare

Hering
herring

Heurige(r)
new wine

Himbeere
raspberry

Hirn
brains

Hirsch
venison

Hummer
lobster

Ingwer
ginger

Jause
snack

Johannisbeere
blackcurrant/
redcurrant

Kalb
calf

Kaldaunen/Kutteln
tripe

Kaltschale
cold sweet soup

Kaninchen
rabbit

Karfiol
cauliflower

Karotten
carrots

Karpfen
carp

Kartoffel
potato

Kartoffelpuffer
potato fritter

Käse
cheese

Kekse
biscuits

Keule
leg

Kirsche
cherry

Klösse (Kartoffel-,
Semmel-)
dumplings (potato,
bread)

Knoblauch
garlic

Knödel
dumplings

Knusprig
crisp/crunchy

Kochschinken
boiled ham

Kompott
stewed fruit/compote

Konfitüre
jam

Korn
corn/corn schnapps

Krabbe
crab

Krapfen
doughnut

Kräuter-
herbal

Labskaus
stew made of meat,
fish and mashed
potato

Lachs
salmon

Languste
crayfish

Lauch
leek

Lebkuchen
gingerbread

Likör
liqueur

Mandel
almond

Marille
apricot

mariniert
marinated

Marone
chestnut

Maultaschen
filled pasta squares

Meerrettich
horseradish

Melone
melon

Mett
minced pork/beef

Milch
milk

Muscheln
mussels

Nockerl
little dumplings

Nougat
nougat

Obst (je nach
Jahreszeit/Saison)
fruit (of the season)

Obstkuchen
fruitcake

Obstler
fruit schnapps

Ochsenschwanz
oxtail

Öl
oil

Orange
orange

Palatschinken
stuffed pancake

Pampelmuse
grapefruit

Pastete
paté

Petersilie
parsley

Pfannkuchen
pancake

Pfeffer
pepper

Pfifferling
chanterelle

Pfirsich
peach

Pflaume
plum

Pilze
mushrooms

Platte
plate

Plätzchen
biscuit/cookie

Pommes frites
French fries

Porree
leek

Preßsack
a type of cold meat

Pute
turkey

Quark
(soft) curd cheese

Radieschen
radish

Rahm
cream

Räucherschinken
smoked ham

Rebhuhn
partridge

Reh
deer

Reibekuchen
potato waffle

Reis
rice

Remoulade
remoulade

resch (rösch)
crisp/crusty

Rinder-
beef

Rinderfilet
beef fillet

Rindfleisch
beef

Rippe
rib

roh
raw

Rosenkohl
Brussels sprouts

Rosine
raisin

Rostbraten
roast

Röstkartoffeln
fried potatoes

rote Beete
beetroot

Rührei
scrambled eggs

Rumpsteak
rump steak

Sachertorte
a rich chocolate cake

Saft
juice

Sahne
cream

Salat (gemischt)
salad (mixed)

Salzkartoffeln
boiled potatoes

Sauerkraut
sauerkraut/pickled
   cabbage

Schaum-
frothy

Schildkrötensuppe
turtle soup

Schinken
ham

Schlagobers
whipped cream

Schmalz
lard

Schmarren
pancake cut up into
   small pieces

Schnecken
escargots

Schnittchen
(Appe-tit)
canapé

Schnittlauch
chives

Schorle
wine and soda
   water mix

Schweinefleisch
pork

Schweinelendchen
small pieces of pork
   loin

Sekt
sparkling wine

Sellerie
celery

Semmel
bread roll

Senf
mustard

Sosse
gravy/sauce

Spanferkel
whole pig roasted over
   an open fire

Spargel
asparagus

Spätzle
spaetzle (type of
   pasta)

Speiseeis
ice-cream

Spinat
spinach

Steinpilz
type of mushroom
   (Boletus edulis)

Strammer Max
open sandwich of boiled ham and fried egg
Strudel
strudel
Süßspeise
sweet dish
Teig (in Öl gebacken)
pastry, batter (baked in oil)
Thunfisch
tuna
Tintenfisch
cuttlefish/squid
Topfen
soft curd cheese
Traube
grape
Truthahn
turkey
Tunke
sauce/gravy

Vesper
a break for eating/cold evening meal
Wachtel
quail
Wald-
forest
Walnuss
walnut
Wein (trocken/mild)
wine (dry/mild)
Wein (süss/ Spätlese/Eiswein)
wine (sweet/late vintage/sweet wine made from grapes which have been exposed to frost)
Wein (Süsswein/ Südwein)
wine (dessert wine/ Mediterranean wine)

Weinbrand
brandy
Weisswurst
veal sausage
Wels
catfish
Würstchen
sausage
Zitrone
lemon
Zunge
tongue
Zwiebel
onion

5. On the road

5.1 Asking for directions

Excuse me, could I ask you something?	Verzeihung, dürfte ich Sie etwas fragen?
	fair tsaioong, duerfter ikh zee etvass frargen?
I've lost my way.	Ich habe mich verlaufen/(with car)mich verfahren.
	ikh harber mikh fairlowfen/mikh fairfahren
Is there a...around here?	Wissen Sie, wo hier in der Nähe ein(e)...ist?
	vissen zee, vo heer in dayr nayher ain(er)... ist?
Is this the way to...?	Ist dies die Strasse nach...?
	ist dees dee shtrasser nakh...?
Could you tell me how to get to...?	Können Sie mir sagen, wie ich nach... (name of the place) fahren/gehen muss?
	koenen zee meer zargen, vee ikh nakh ...fahren/gayhen muss?
What's the quickest way to...?	Wie komme ich am schnellsten nach...?
	vee kommer ikh am shnellsten nakh...?

geradeaus	**überqueren**	**der Fluss**
straight	cross	the river
nach links/links	**die Kreuzung**	**die Brücke**
abbiegen	the intersection	the bridge
left/turn left	**die Strasse**	**die (Bahn)schranken**
nach rechts/rechts	the street	the level crossing/the
abbiegen	**die (Verkehrs)**	boomgates
right/turn right	**ampel**	**das Schild**
abbiegen	the traffic light	**Richtung...**
turn	**das Gebäude**	the sign pointing to ...
folgen	the building	**der Pfeil**
follow	**an der Ecke**	the arrow
	at the corner	

Ich weiss nicht, ich kenne mich hier nicht aus.	I don't know, I don't know my way around here.
Da sind Sie hier nicht richtig.	You're going the wrong way.
Sie müssen zurück nach...	You have to go back to...
Sie fahren über die...Strasse.	You take...Street.
Sie fahren über die...Strasse drüber.	You cross over...Street.
Da sehen Sie schon die Schilder.	From there you will see the signs.
Da müssen Sie noch mal fragen.	When you get there, you will have to ask again.

How many kilometres is it to...?

Wieviel Kilometer sind es noch bis...?
veefeel kilomayter zint ez nokh biss...?

Could you point it out on the map?

Können Sie es mir auf der Karte zeigen?
koennen zee ez meer owf dayr karter tsaigen?

5.2 Customs

● **Border documents:** along with your passport you must carry your original documents with you. These include your valid full driving licence (together with paper counterpart if photocard licence), vehicle registration document and motor insurance certificate.

Contact your motor insurer for advice at least a month before taking your vehicle overseas to ensure that you are adequately covered. A warning triangle must be carried and a first-aid kit and a set of replacement bulbs are recommended.

For further information on driving in Germany visit theAA.com/motoring_advice/overseas

Ihren Pass bitte.	Your passport, please.
Die grüne Karte bitte.	Your green card, please.
Ihre Fahrzeugpapiere bitte.	Your vehicle documents, please.
Ihr Visum bitte.	Your visa, please.
Wohin fahren Sie?	Where are you heading?
Wie lange bleiben Sie/halten Sie sich dort auf?	How long are you planning to stay?
Haben Sie etwas zu verzollen?	Do you have anything to declare?
Würden Sie dies bitte öffnen?	Open this, please.

I'm travelling through.
Ich bin auf der Durchreise.
ikh bin owf dayr doorkh raizer

I'm going on holiday to…
Ich fahre in den Urlaub nach...
ikh fahrer in den oorlowp nakh...

I'm on a business trip.
Ich bin auf Geschäftsreise.
ikh bin owf geshefts-raizer

I don't know how long I'll be staying yet.
Ich weiss noch nicht, wie lange ich bleibe.
ikh vaiss nokh nikht, vee langer ikh blaiber

I'll be staying here for a weekend.
Ich bleibe hier übers Wochenende.
ikh blaiber heer uebers vokhen ender

– for a few days.
Ich bleibe hier ein paar Tage.
ikh blaiber heer ain par targer

– for a week.
Ich bleibe hier eine Woche.
ikh blaiber heer ainer vokher

–for two weeks.
Ich bleibe hier zwei Wochen.
ikh blaiber heer tsvai vokhen

I've got nothing to declare.
Ich habe nichts zu verzollen.
ikh harber nikhts tsoo fairtsollen

I've got...with me.
Ich habe ... mit.
ikh harber ... mit

– a carton of cigarettes.
Ich habe eine Stange Zigaretten.
ikh harber ainer shtanger tseegaretten

– a bottle of...	Ich habe eine Flasche...
	ikh harber ainer flusher...
– some souvenirs.	Ich habe ein paar Andenken.
	ikh harber ain par andenken
These are personal effects.	Das sind persönliche Sachen.
	dass zint perzoenlikher zakhen
These are not new.	Diese Sachen sind nicht neu.
	deezer zakhen zint nikht noy
Here's the receipt.	Hier ist der (Kassen)zettel.
	heer ist dayr (kassen)tsettel
This is for private use.	Das ist für den eigenen Gebrauch.
	dass ist fuer dayn aigenen gebrowkh
How much import duty do I have to pay?	Wieviel Einfuhrzoll muss ich zahlen?
	veefeel ainfoor-tsoll muss ikh tsarlen?
Can I go now?	Darf ich jetzt gehen?
	darf ikh yetst gayhen?

5.3 Luggage

Porter!	Gepäckträger!
	gepeck-trayger!
Could you take this luggage to...?	Würden Sie dieses Gepäck zu/in...bringen?
	vuerden zee deezes gepek tsoo/in ...bringen?
How much do I owe you?	Wieviel bekommen Sie von mir?
	veefeel bekommen zee fon meer?
Where can I find a luggage trolley?	Wo kann ich eine Gepäckkarre finden?
	vo kann ikh ainer gepek-karrer finden?
Could you store this luggage for me?	Kann ich dieses Gepäck zur Aufbewahrung abgeben?
	kann ikh deezes gepek tsoor owfbevahrung apgayben?
Where are the luggage lockers?	Wo sind die Schliessfächer?
	vo zint dee shleess-fekher?

I can't get the locker open.	Ich bekomme das Schliessfach nicht auf.
	ikh bekommer dass shleessfakh nikht owf
How much is it per item per day?	Wieviel kostet es je Stück pro Tag?
	veefeel kostet es yay shtuek pro tark?
This is not my bag/suitcase.	Das ist nicht meine Tasche/mein Koffer.
	dass ist nikht mainer tasher/main koffer
There's one item/bag/ suitcase missing still.	Es fehlt noch ein Stück/eine Tasche/ ein Koffer.
	ez faylt nokh ain shtuek/ayner tasher/ ain koffer
My suitcase is damaged.	Mein Koffer ist beschädigt
	main koffer ist beshaydikt

5.4 Traffic signs

abbiegen	**Durchgangsverkehr**	**Glatteis**
turn	**(verboten)**	ice on road
Anlieger frei	(no) throughway	**Kurve(nreiche**
residents only	**Einbahnstrasse**	**Strecke)**
Auffahrt	one way street	bend/dangerous
slip road/approach	**Einfahrt**	bends
to house	entry/access	**Licht einschalten/**
Auflieger schwenkt	**Ende der Autobahn**	**ausschalten**
aus	end of motorway	switch on lights/end of
trailer may swing out	**Frostaufbrüche**	need for lights
Ausfahrt	frost damage	**LKW**
exit	**Gefahr**	heavy goods vehicle
Autobahndreieck	danger	**Naturschutzgebiet**
motorway merging	**gefährlich**	nature reserve
point	dangerous	**Nebel**
Baustelle	**Gegenverkehr**	beware fog
road works ahead	oncoming traffic	**Parkscheibe**
bei Nässe/Glätte	**gesperrt (für alle**	parking disk
in wet/icy conditions	**Fahrzeuge)**	**PKW**
	closed (for all vehicles)	motorcar

Radfahrer kreuzen
cyclists crossing
Rasthof-stätte
services
Rastplatz bitte
  sauberhalten
please keep picnic
  area tidy
Rollsplit
loose chippings
Schleudergefahr
danger of skidding
Seitenstreifen nicht
  befahrbar
soft verges
Seitenwind
crosswind
Spurrillen
irregular road surface
Standstreifen
hard shoulder
Starkes Gefälle
steep hill

Stau
traffic jam
Stauwarnanlage
hazard lights
Steinschlag
falling stones
Talbrücke
bridge over a valley
Überholverbot
no overtaking
Umleitung
diversion
Unbeschränkter
  Bahnübergang
unguarded level
  crossing/dangerous
  crossing
Verengte Fahrbahn
narrow lane
Vorfahrt beachten
give way
Vorfahrtsstrasse
major road

Wasserschutzgebiet
protected reservoir
  area
zurückschalten
to change back

5.5 The car

Maximum speed for cars:
130km/h on motorways
100km/h outside built-up areas
50km/h in built-up areas

Give way: on roads without yellow diamond priority signs, give way to
traffic from the right. Give way to pedestrians when turning right or left at
uncontrolled junctions (intersections). Traffic lights are supplemented by
priority signs, which must be obeyed when the lights are not functioning.

The parts of the car

battery	der Akku/die Batterie	dayr akoo/batteree
rear light	das Rücklicht	dass ruekleekht
rear-view mirror	der Rückspiegel	dayr ruekshpeegell
reversing light	der Rückfahrscheinwerfer	dayr rueckfahr-shaynverfer
aerial	die Antenne	dee antennar
car radio	das Autoradio	dass owtorardiyoo
petrol tank	der Benzintank	dayr bentseentank
inside mirror	der Innenspiegel	dayr innen-shpeegel
sparking plugs	die Zündkerze(n)	dee tsuentkairtsen
fuel filter/pump	das Treibstofffilter/die Triebstoffpumpe	dass traipshtofffilter/dee traip-shtoffpoomper
wing mirror	der Aussenspiegel	dayr owsen-shpeegel
bumper	die Stoßstange	dee shtoass-shtanger
carburettor	der Vergaser	dayr fairgarzer
crankcase	das Kurbelgehäuse	dass koorbellgehoyzer
cylinder	der Zylinder	dayr tsilinder
ignition	die Zündung	dee tsuendoong
warning light	die Kontrollampe	dee kontroal-lamper
dynamo	der Dynamo	dayr deenamo
accelerator	das Gaspedal	dass gas-pedarl
handbrake	die Handbremse	dee hantbremzer
valve	das Ventil	dass venteel
silencer	der Auspufftopf	dayr owspuff-topf
boot	der Kofferraum	dayr kofferrowm
headlight	der Scheinwerfer	dayr shaynverfer
crank shaft	die Kurbelwelle	dee koorbelveller
air filter	das Luftfilter	dass looft-filter
fog lamp	die Nebelleuchte	dee naybel-loykhter
engine block	der Motorblock	dayr moatorblock
camshaft	die Nockenwelle	dee nokkenveller

oil filter/pump	das Ölfilter/	*dass oelfilter/dee*
	die Ölpump	*oelpoomper*
dipstick	der Ölstandstab	*dayr oel-shtunt-shtarp*
pedal	das Pedal	*dass pedarl*
door	die Wagentür	*dee vargentuer*
radiator	der Kühler	*dayr kuehler*
brake disc	die Bremsscheibe	*dee bremz-shayber*
spare wheel	das Ersatzrad	*dass erzatsrart*
indicator	der Blinker	*dayr blinker*
windscreen wiper	der Scheibenwischer	*dayr shaibenvisher*
shock absorbers	der Stossdämpfer	*dayr shtossdempfer*
sunroof	das Schiebdach	*dass sheebedakh*
spoiler	der Spoiler	*dayr shpoyler*
starter motor	der Startmotor	*dayr shtartmoator*
steering column	die Lenksäule	*dee lenkzoyler*
exhaust pipe	das Auspuffrohr	*dass owspoofrohr*
seat belt	der Sicherheitsgurt	*dayr zikher-haitsgoort*
fan	der Ventilator	*dayr venteelator*
distributor cables	das Verteilerkabel	*dass fertailer-karbel*
gear lever	der Schalthebel	*dayr shalt-haybel*
windscreen	die Windschutzscheibe	*dee vintshoots-shaiber*
water pump	die Wasserpumpe	*dee vasserpoomper*
wheel	das Rad	*dass rart*
hubcap	die Radkappe	*dee rartkapper*
piston	der Kolben	*dayr kolben*

5.6 The petrol station

How many kilometres to the next petrol station, please?

Wieviel Kilometer sind es bis zur nächsten Tankstelle?

veefeel kilomayter zint ez biss tsoor nexten tankshteller?

I would like...litres of..., please.

Ich möchte...Liter.

ikh moekhter ...liter

– leaded.

Ich möchte...Liter normal (es Bezin).

ikh moekhter...liter normarl (ez bentseen)

– unleaded.

Ich möchte...Liter bleifrei (es Benzin).

ikh moekhter...liter blaifrai (ez bentseen)

– diesel.

Ich möchte...Liter Diesel.

ikh moekhter...liter deezel

I would like... euros worth of petrol, please.

Ich möchte für...euros (Auto)gas.

ikh moekhter fuer...euros (owto)gass

Fill it up, please.

Voll bitte.

foll bitter

Could you check...?

Würden Sie bitte...kontrollieren?

vuerden zee bitter...kontrolleeren?

– the oil level.

Kontrollieren Sie bitte den Ölstand.

kontrolleeren zee bitter dayn oelshtant

– the tyre pressure.

Kontrollieren Sie bitte den Reifendruck.

kontrolleeren zee bitter dayn raifendrukk

Could you change the oil, please?

Wechseln Sie bitte das Öl.

vekhseln zee bitter dass oel

Could you clean the windows/ the windscreen, please?

Reinigen Sie bitte die Windschutzscheibe.

rainigen zee bitter dee vint-shoots-shaiber

Could you give the car a wash, please?

Kann ich hier mein Auto waschen lassen?

kann ikh main owto heer vashen lassen?

5.7 Breakdown and repairs

I'm having car trouble. Could you give me a hand?	Ich habe eine Panne. Können Sie mir helfen?
	ikh harber ainer panner. koennen zee meer helfen?
I've run out of petrol.	Ich habe kein Benzin mehr.
	ikh harber kain bentseen mayr
I've locked the keys in the car.	Ich habe die Schlüssel im Auto steckenlassen.
	ikh harber dee shluessel im owto shtekken lassen
The car/motorbike/moped won't start.	Das Auto/Motorrad/Moped springt nicht an.
	dass owto/moator rat/moapet shprinkt nikht an
Could you contact the recovery service for me, please?	Könnten Sie für mich die Pannenhilfe benachrichtigen?
	koennten zee fuer mikh dee pannen-hilfer benakh-rikhtigen?
Could you call a garage for me, please?	Könnten Sie für mich eine Werkstatt anrufen?
	koennten zee fuer mikh ainer vairkshtatt anroofen?
Could you give me a lift to...?	Darf ich mit Ihnen nach...mitfahren?
	darf ikh mit eenen nakh...mitfahren?
– a garage/into town?	Darf ich mit Ihnen bis zu einer Werkstatt/ in die Stadt mitfahren?
	darf ikh mit eenen biss tsoo ainer verkshtatt/in dee shtatt mit fahren?
– a phone booth?	Darf ich mit Ihnen bis zu einer Telefonzelle mitfahren?
	darf ikh mit eenen biss tsoo ainer tellefoan tseller mit fahren?

– an emergency phone?	Darf ich mit Ihnen bis zu einer Rufsäule mitfahren?
	darf ikh mit eenen biss tsoo ainer roofzoyler mit fahren?
Can we take my bicycle/moped?	Kann mein Fahrrad/Moped auch mit?
	kann main fahr rat/moapet owkh mit?
Could you tow me to a garage?	Könnten Sie mich zu einer Werkstatt (ab) schleppen?
	koennten zee mikh tsoo ainer verkshtatt (ap)shleppen?
There's probably something wrong with... *(See pages 72–73)*	Wahrscheinlich ist mit dem/der/ den... etwas nicht in Ordnung.
	varshainlikh ist mit daym/dayr/dayn ...etvass nikht in ordnoong
Can you fix it?	Können Sie es reparieren?
	koennen zee es repareeren?
Could you fix my tyre?	Können Sie den Reifen flicken?
	koennen zee dayn raifen flikken?
Could you change this wheel?	Können Sie das Rad wechseln?
	koennen zee dass rart vekhzeln?
Can you fix it so it'll get me to...?	Können Sie es soweit reparieren, dass ich damit nach...fahren kann?
	koennen zee es zovait repareeren dass ikh darmit nakh...fahren kann?
Which garage can help me?	Welche Werkstatt kann mir denn dann helfen?
	velkher verkshtatt kann meer denn dann helfen?
When will my car/bicycle be ready?	Wann ist mein Auto/Fahrrad fertig?
	vann ist main owto/fahr rart fairtikh?
Can I wait for it here?	Kann ich hier darauf warten?
	kann ikh heer darrowf varten?
How much will it cost?	Wieviel wird es kosten?
	veefeel virt es kosten?

Could you itemise the bill?	Können Sie die Rechnung spezifizieren?
	koennen zee dee rekhnoong shpetsi-fitseeren?
Can I have a receipt for the insurance?	Ich hätte gern eine Quittung für die Versicherung?
	ikh hetter gayrn ainer kvittoong fuer dee fairzikheroong

5.8 The bicycle/moped

● Cycle paths are common in towns and cities and their use is strongly recommended. Bikes can usually be hired at tourist centres. The maximum speed for mopeds is 40km/h both inside and outside town centres. Crash helmets are compulsory.

Ich habe keine Ersatzteile für Ihren Wagen/Ihr Fahrrad	I don't have parts for your car/ bicycle
Ich muss die Ersatzteile irgendwo anders besorgen	I have to get the parts from somewhere else
Ich muss die Ersatzteile bestellen	I have to order the parts
Das dauert einen halben Tag	That'll take half a day
Das dauert einen Tag	That'll take a day
Das dauert ein paar Tage	That'll take a few days
Das dauert eine Woche	That'll take a week
Ihr Auto ist schrottreif	Your car is a write-off
Hier ist nichts mehr zu machen	It can't be repaired.
Das Auto/Motorrad/Moped/ Fahrrad ist um...Uhr fertig.	The car/motor bike/moped/ bicycle will be ready at...o'clock.

The parts of a bike

rear lamp	das Rücklicht	*dass rueklikht*
rear wheel	das Hinterrad	*dass hinter-rart*
(luggage) carrier	der Gepäckträger	*dayr gepektrayger*
bicycle fork	das Steuer(kopf)rohr	*dass shtoyer(kopf)rohr*
bell	die Klingel	*dee klingel*
inner tube	der Schlauch	*dayr shlowkh*
tyre	der Reifen	*dayr raifen*
crank	die Kurbel	*dee koorbel*
gear change	der Umwerfer	*dayr oomverfer*
wire	das Kabel	*dass karbel*
dynamo	der Dynamo	*dayr deenamo*
bicycle trailer	der Fahrradanhänger	*dayr fahr-rartanhenger*
frame	der Rahmen	*dayr rarmen*
dress guard	der Kleiderschutz	*dayr klaidershoots*
chain	die Kette	*dee ketter*
chain guard	der Kettenschutz	*dayr kettenshoots*
chain lock	das Kettenschloss	*dass kettenshloss*
milometer	der Kilometerzähler	*dayr keelomaytertsayler*
child's seat	der Kindersitz	*dayr kinderzits*
headlamp	der Scheinwerfer	*dayr shainverfer*
bulb	die Birne	*dee beerner*
pedal	das Pedal	*dass pedarl*
pump	die Pumpe	*dee poomper*
reflector	der Rückstrahler	*dayr ruek-shtrarler*
break pad	die Bremsbacke	*dee bremzbakker*
brake cable	das Bremskabel	*dass bremzkarbel*
ring lock	das Sicherheitsschloss	*dass zikherhaits-shloss*
carrier straps	das Spannband	*dass shpannbant*
tachometer	der Tacho(meter)	*dayr takhomayter*
spoke	die Speiche	*die shpaikher*
mudguard	das Schutzblech	*dass shootsblekh*

handlebar	der Lenker	*dayr lenker*
chain wheel	das Zahnrad	*dass tsarnrart*
toe clip	der Rennhaken	*dayr renharken*
crank axle	die Tretwelle	*dee traytveller*
drum brake	die Trommelbremse	*dee trommel-bremzer*
rim	die Felge	*dee felger*
valve	das Ventil	*dass venteel*
valve tube	der Ventilschlauch	*dayr venteel-shlowkh*
gear cable	das Gangschaltungs-kabel	*dass gangshaltoongskarbel*
fork	die Vorderradgabel	*dee forder-rartgarbel*
front wheel	das Vorderrad	*dass forderrart*
seat	der Sattel	*dayr zattel*

5.9 Renting a vehicle

I'd like to rent a...	Ich möchte ein(en)...mieten.
	ikh moekhter ain(en)...meeten
Do I need a (special) licence for that?	Brauche ich dafür einen (bestimmten) Führerschein?
	browkher ikh dafuer ainen (beshtimmten) fuehrershain?
I'd like to rent the...for...	Ich möchte den/das...für...mieten.
	ikh moekhter dayn/dass...fuer...meeten
– one day.	Ich möchte den/das...für einen Tag mieten.
	ikh moekhter dayn/dass...fuer ainen tark meeten
– two days.	Ich möchte den/das ...für zwei Tage mieten.
	ikh moekhter dayn/dass...fuer tsvai targer meeten
How much is that per day/week?	Wieviel kostet das pro Tag/Woche?
	veefeel kostet dass pro tark/vokher?
How much is the deposit?	Wie hoch ist die Kaution?
	vee hokh ist dee kowtseeoan?
Could I have a receipt for the deposit?	Geben Sie mir bitte eine Quittung, dass ich die Kaution bezahlt habe?
	gayben zee meer bitter ainer kvittoong, dass ikh dee kowtseeoan betsarlt harber
How much is the surcharge per kilometre?	Wie hoch ist der zusätzliche Kilometerpreis?
	vee hokh ist dayr tsoo zetslikher kilo-mayter praiss?
Does that include petrol?	Ist das Benzin mit enthalten?
	ist dass bentseen mit enthalten?

Does that include insurance?	Ist die Versicherung mit enthalten?
	ist dee fairsikhe roong mit enthalten?
What time can I pick the...up tomorrow?	Wann kann ich das...morgen abholen?
	vann kann ikh dass...morgen apholen?
When does the... have to be back?	Wann muss ich den/das... zurückbringen?
	vann mooss ikh dayn/dass ...tsooruekbringen?
Where's the petrol tank?	Wo ist der Tank?
	vo ist dayr tank?
What sort of fuel does it take?	Was muss ich tanken?
	vass mooss ikh tanken?

6. Public transport

6.1 In general

● Public transport in Germany prides itself for being on time. Strikes (*Streiks*) are rare and only tend to occur around the trade unions' negotiations on pay which take place once a year. Tickets for buses can be bought as you get on the bus. Some unlimited travel cards/ runabout tickets purchased for use on trains also cover all public means of transport within a designated area (*Verkehrsverbund*). Train tickets can be purchased either at the ticket office in the station or at ticket machines on the platforms.

Announcements

Der Zug nach...von...hat eine Verspätung von...Minuten.	The train to...from has been delayed by...minutes.
Auf Gleis ... fährt ein der Zug nach.../aus...	The train now arriving at platform... is the train to.../from...
Auf Gleis...steht der Zug zur Abfahrt bereit nach...	The train to...is about to leave from platform...
Achtung! Bitte zurückbleiben! Ein Intercity fährt durch auf Gleis...	Attention please, keep your distance from the rail track, an intercity train will pass on platform...
Wir nähern uns (der Station/dem Hauptbahnhof)...	We're now approaching...(the station/ main station).

Where does this train go to?	Wohin fährt dieser Zug?
	vohinn fairt deezer tsook?
Does this boat go to...?	Fährt dieses Schiff nach...?
	fairt deezes shiff nakh...?
Can I take this bus to...?	Kann ich mit diesem Bus nach...fahren?
	kann ikh mitt deezem boos nakh ...fahren?

Does this train stop at...?	Hält dieser Zug in...?
	helt deezer tsook in...?
Is this seat taken/ free/reserved?	Ist dieser Platz besetzt/frei/reserviert?
	ist deezer plats bezetst/frai/rezerveert?
I've booked...	Ich habe...reservieren lassen.
	ikh haber...rezerveeren lassen
Could you tell me where I have to get off for... ?	Könnten Sie mir sagen, wo ich aussteigen muss, um zu/zum/zur/zu den ... zu kommen?
	koennten zee meer zargen, vo ikh ows shtaigen mooss, oom tsoo/tsoom/ tsoor/tsoo dayn...tsoo kommen?
Could you let me know when we get to...?	Würden Sie mir bitte Bescheid sagen, wenn wir bei/beim/bei der/bei den... sind?
	vuerden zee meer bitter beshait zargen, venn veer bai/baim/bai dayr/bai dayn ...zint?
Could you stop at the next stop, please?	Halten Sie bitte an der nächsten Haltestelle
	halten zee bitter an dayr nexten halter shteller
Where are we now?	Wo sind wir hier?
	vo zint veer heer?
Do I have to get off here?	Muss ich hier aussteigen?
	mooss ikh heer ows shtaigen?
Have we already passed...?	Sind wir schon an/am/an der...vorbei?
	zint veer shoan an/am/an dayr...forbai?
How long have I been asleep?	Wie lange habe ich geschlafen?
	vee langer harber ikh geshlarfen?
How long does…stop here?	Wie lange bleibt der/die...hier stehen?
	vee langer blaipt dayr/dee...heer shtayhen?
Can I come back on the same ticket?	Kann ich mit dieser Fahrkarte auch wieder zurück?
	kann ikh mit deezer farkarter owkh veeder tsooruek?

Can I change on this ticket?	Kann ich mit dieser Fahrkarte umsteigen?
	kann ikh mit deezer farkarter oomshtaigen?
How long is this ticket valid for?	Wie lange ist diese Fahrkarte gültig?
	vee langer ist deezer farkarter gueltikh?
How much is the supplement for the intercity (high speed train)?	Wie hoch ist der IC Zuschlag?
	vee hokh ist der ee tsee tsooschlark?

6.2 Questions to passengers

Ticket types

Erster oder zweiter Klasse?	First or second class?
Einfach oder hin und zurück/ Hin- und Rückfahrt?	Single or return?
Raucher oder Nichtraucher?	Smoking or non-smoking?
Am Fenster oder am Gang?	Window or aisle?
Vorn oder hinten?	Front or back?
Sitzplatz oder Liegewagen?	Seat or couchette?
Oben, in der Mitte oder unten?	Top, middle or bottom?
Touristenklasse oder Business Class?	Tourist class or business class?
Kabine oder Sitzplatz?	Cabin or seat?
Einzel- oder Doppelkabine?	Single or double?
Zu wieviel Personen reisen Sie?	How many are travelling?

Destination

Wohin reisen Sie?	Where are you travelling to?
Wann reisen Sie ab?	When are you leaving?
Abfahrt/Abflug (aircraft) um...	Your...leaves at...
Sie müssen in...umsteigen.	You have to change trains at...
Sie müssen in...aussteigen.	You have to get off at...
Sie müssen über...reisen.	You have to travel via...
Die Hinreise fängt am...an.	The outward journey is on...
Die Rückreise beginnt am...	The return journey is on...
Sie müssen spätestens... an Bord sein	You have to be on board by...

Inside the vehicle

Ihre Fahrkarte bitte.	Your ticket, please.
Ihre Reservierung bitte.	Your reservation, please.
Ihren (Reise)pass bitte.	Your passport, please.
Sie sitzen im/in der falschen...	You're on/in the wrong.
Sie sitzen auf dem falschen Platz	You're in the wrong seat.
Dieser Platz ist reserviert	This seat is reserved.
Sie müssen einen Zuschlag (be) zahlen.	You'll have to pay a supplement.
Der/die/das...hat eine Verspätung von ...Minuten	The...has been delayed by... minutes.

6.3 Tickets

Where can I...?	Wo kann ich...?
	vo kann ikh...?
– buy a ticket?	Wo kann ich eine Karte kaufen?
	vo kann ikh ainer karter kowfen?
– make a reservation?	Wo kann ich einen Platz reservieren lassen?
	vo kann ikh ainen plats rezerveeren lassen?
– book a flight?	Wo kann ich einen Flug buchen?
	vo kann ikh ainen flook bookhen?
Could I have a...to..., please?	Ich möchte...nach...
	ikh moekhter...nakh...
– a single	Ich möchte einmal einfach nach...
	ikh moekhter ainmarl ainfakh nakh...
– a return	Ich möchte eine Rückfahrkarte nach...
	ikh moekhter ainer ruekfarkarter nakh...
first class	erster Klasse
	airster klasser
second class	zweiter Klasse
	tsvaiter klasser
tourist class	Touristen-klasse
	tooristen klasser
business class	Business Class
	bizniss klarss
I'd like to book a seat/couchette/cabin.	Ich möchte einen Sitzplatz/Liegewagenplatz/eine Kabine reservieren lassen.
	ikh moekhter ainen zits-plats/leeger vargen plats/ainer kabiner rezerveeren
I'd like to book a berth in the sleeping car.	Ich möchte einen Platz im Schlafwagen reservieren lassen.
	ikh moekhter ainen plats im shlarfvargen rezerveeren lassen.
top/middle/bottom	oben/in der Mitte/unten
	oaben/in dayr mitter/oonten

smoking/no smoking	Raucher/Nichtraucher
	rowkher/nikht rowkher
by the window	am Fenster
	am fenster
single/double	Einzel-/Doppel-
	aintsel-/doppel-
at the front/back	vorn/hinten
	forn/hinten
There are...of us.	Wir sind zu ...t (e.g. zweit, dritt, viert)
	veer zint tsoo ...t (e.g. tsvait, dritt, feert)
a car	ein Auto
	ain owto
a caravan	ein Wohnwagen
	ain voanvargen
...bicycles	...Fahr-räder
	...fahr rayder
Do you also have...?	Haben Sie...?
	harben zee...?
– season tickets?	Haben Sie Sammelfahrscheine?
	harben zee zammel-fahr-shainer?
– weekly tickets?	Haben Sie Wochenkarten?
	harben zee vokhen-karten?
– monthly season tickets?	Haben Sie Monatskarten?
	harben zee moanarts-karten?

6.4 Information

Where's?	Wo ist...?
	vo ist...?
Where's the information desk?	Wo ist die Auskunft?
	vo ist dee owskoonft?
Where can I find a timetable?	Wo ist die Tafel mit den Abfahrtszeiten/ Ankunftszeiten?
	vo ist dee tarfel mit den apfahrts-tsaiten/ ankunfts-tsaiten?

Where's the...desk?	Wo ist der Schalter für...?
	vo ist dayr shalter fuer...?
Do you have a city map with routes on it?	Haben Sie einen Stadtplan mit dem Bus/ the bus/the underground U-Bahnnetz?
	harben zee ainen shtatplarn mit dem booss-/oobarn nets?
Do you have a timetable?	Haben Sie einen Fahrplan?
	harben zee ainen farplarn?
I'd like to confirm/cancel/ change my booking for...	Ich möchte meine Reservierung/Reise nach...bestätigen/annullieren/ändern
	ikh moekhter mainer rezerveerung/raizer nakh ...beshtaytigen/annoo-leeren/ endern
Will I get my money back?	Bekomme ich mein Geld zurück?
	bekommer ikh main gelt tsooruek?
I want to go to...How do I get there? (What's the quickest way there?)	Ich muss nach... Wie komme ich da (am schnellsten) hin?
	ikh mooss nakh ...vee kommer ikh da (am shnellsten) hin?
How much is a single/return to...?	Wieviel kostet eine Fahrt/Rückfahrkarte nach...?
	veefeel kostet ainer fart/ruek-fahr-karter nakh...?
Do I have to pay a supplement?	Muss ich Zuschlag zahlen?
	mooss ikh tsooshlak tsarlen?
Can I interrupt my journey with this ticket?	Darf ich die Reise mit diesem Ticket unterbrechen?
	darf ikh dee raizer mit deezem ticket oonter-brekhen?
How much luggage am I allowed?	Wieviel Gepäck darf ich mitnehmen?
	veefeel gepeck darf ikh mitnaymen?
Does this...travel direct?	Geht diese(r)/dieses ... direkt?
	gayt deeze(r)/deezes ... direkt?
Do I have to change? Where?	Muss ich umsteigen? Wo?
	mooss ikh oom-shtaigen? vo?

Will this plane make any stopovers?	Macht das Flugzeug eine Zwischenlandung?
	makht dass flooktsoyk ainer tsvishen-landoong?
Does the boat call in at any ports on the way?	Legt das Schiff unterwegs in irgendwelchen Häfen an?
	laykt dass shiff oontervegz in eergent-velkhen hayfen an?
Does the train/bus stop at...?	Hält der Zug/Bus in...?
	helt der tsook/booss in...?
Where should I get off?	Wo muss ich aussteigen?
	vo mooss ikh ows-shtaigen?
Is there a connection to...?	Gibt es einen Anschluss nach...?
	gipt ez ainen anschluss nakh...?
How long do I have to wait?	Wie lange muss ich warten?
	vee langer mooss ikh varten?
When does...leave?	Wann fährt...ab?
	vann fairt...ap?
What time does the first/next/last...leave?	Wann fährt/fliegt (aircraft) der/die/das erste/nächste/letzte...?
	vann fairt/fleekt dayr/dee/dass airster/nexter/letster...?
How long does...take?	Wie lange dauert die Fahrt/der Flug (flight)?
	vee langer dowert dee fahrt/dayr flook?
What time does...arrive in...?	Wann kommt...in...an?
	vann kommt...in...an?
Where does the...to...leave from?	Wo fährt/(aircraft) fliegt der/die/das nach ...ab?
	vo fairt/fleekt dayr/dee/duss nakh...ap?
Is this...to...?	Ist dies...nach...?
	ist deez...nakh...?

6.5 Aeroplanes

● On arrival at a German airport (*Flughafen*), you will find the following signs:

Abflug Inland/Ausland	Ankunft
domestic/international departures	arrivals

After the check-in a boarding pass (*Bordkarte, Einsteigekarte*) is handed out which details the gate (*Flugsteig*) and departure time (*Abflugzeit*).

6.6 Trains

● The rail network is extensive. The Deutsche Bundesbahn is responsible for the national rail traffic. Generally there are four types of trains: *Intercity, Eilzug/Schnellzug* (fast train which does not stop at small stations - long distance), *S-Bahn* (designed to link smaller towns and villages on the outskirts with the city centre), *U-Bahn* (underground). A supplement is only to be paid for the *Intercity*. Seats can be reserved in advance on the *Intercity* and *Eilzug* only.

6.7 Taxis

● In nearly all large cities and bigger towns, there are plenty of taxis. Although German taxis have no fixed colour, they tend to be cream coloured. Virtually all taxis have a meter.

Besetzt	Taxistand	Frei
booked	taxi rank	for hire

Taxi! | Taxi!
| *tarksi!*

Could you get me a taxi, please? | Würden Sie mir bitte ein Taxi/eine Taxe bestellen?
| *vuerden zee meer bitter ain tarksi/ainer tarkser beshtellen?*

Where can I find a taxi around here? | Wo finde ich hier in der Nähe ein Taxi?
| *vo finder ikh heer in dayr nayher ain tarksi?*

Could you take me to..., please? | Zu/zum/zur...bitte.
| *tsoo/tsoom/tsoor...bitter.*

– this address. | Zu dieser Adresse bitte.
| *tsoo deezer adresser bitter.*

– the...hotel. | Zum Hotel...bitte.
| *tsoom hotel...bitter.*

– the town/city centre. | Ins Zentrum bitte.
| *ins tsentroom bitter.*

– the station. | Zum Bahnhof bitte.
| *tsoom barnhoaf bitter.*

– the airport. | Zum Flughafen bitte.
| *tsoom flook harfen bitter.*

How much is the trip to...? | Wieviel kostet die Fahrt zu/zum/zur...?
| *veefeel kostet dee fart tsoo/tsoom/tsoor...?*

How far is it to...? | Wie weit ist es nach...?
| *vee vait ist ez nakh...?*

Could you turn on the meter, please? | Würden Sie bitte das Taxameter einschalten?
| *vuerden zee bitter dass taksarmeter ainshalten?*

I'm in a hurry. | Ich habe es eilig.
| *ikh haber ez ailikh*

Could you speed up/slow down a little? | Könnten Sie etwas schneller/langsamer fahren?
| *koennten zee etvass shneller/langzarmer fahren?*

Could you take a different route?	Könnten Sie eine andere Strecke fahren?
	koennten zee ainer anderer shtrekker fahren?
I'd like to get out here, please.	Lassen Sie mich hier aussteigen.
	lassen zee mikh heer owsshtaigen
You have to go...	Sie müssen gehen...
	zee muessen gayhen...
– straight on here.	hier geradeaus
	heer gerarder ows
– turn left here.	hier (nach) links
	heer (nakh) links
– turn right here.	hier (nach) rechts
	heer (nakh) rekhts
This is it.	Hier ist es
	heer ist ez
Could you wait a minute for me, please?	Warten Sie bitte einen Augenblick.
	varten zee bitter ainen owgenblick

7. Overnight accommodation

7.1 General

● There is a great variety of overnight accommodation in Germany.
Hotels: the 'star-system' does not tend to be operational in Germany.
However, some are hotels '*vom ADAC empfohlen*' (recommended by the
German motoring organisation) promising good standard. Most hotels
offer *Halbpension* (half board) or *Vollpension* (full board).
Pension/Gasthof/Gästehaus: often smaller houses with B&B type
accommodation. A *Gasthof* would also have a restaurant.
Rasthof: accommodation available at motorway service stations.
Ferienwohnungen: holiday flats available in many tourist places,
recreational centres and/or camping sites.
Berghütten: mountain hut providing basic sleeping space.
Jugendherberge: Youth Hostels in Germany require an international
Youth Hostel pass and usually expect clients to provide their own linen.
Campingplatz: free camping is not allowed in Germany. Camping sites
are usually privately run and not open all year round.

Wie lange bleiben Sie?	How long will you be staying?
Würden Sie bitte das Formular ausfüllen?	Fill out this form, please.
Dürfte ich bitte Ihren Pass haben?	Could I see your passport?
Sie müssen eine Kaution stellen/zahlen.	I'll need a deposit.
Sie müssen im voraus (be)zahlen.	You'll have to pay in advance.
Ich brauche Ihre Kreditkarteninformationen.	I'll need your credit card details.

My name's...I've made a reservation over the phone/by mail/by email

Mein Name ist...Ich habe einen Platz reservieren lassen (telefonisch/schriftlich/online)

main narmer ist...ikh harber ainen plats rezerveeren lassen (telefoanish/shriftlikh/onlain)

How much is it per night/week/ month?

Wieviel kostet es pro Nacht/Woche/Monat?

veefeel kostet ez pro nakht/vokher/moanart?

We'll be staying at least... nights/weeks.

Wir bleiben mindestens...Nächte/Wochen.

veer blaiben mindestens...nekhter/vokhen

We don't know yet.

Das wissen wir noch nicht genau.

dass vissen veer nokh nikht genow

Do you allow pets (cats/dogs)?

Sind Haustiere (Hunde/Katzen) erlaubt?

zint howzteerer (hunder/katsen) erlowpt?

What time does the gate/door open/close?

Wann ist die Pforte/Tür geöffnet/(auf)/geschlossen/(zu)?

van ist dee pforter/tuer geoeffnet/(owf)/geshlossen/(tsoo)?

Could you get me a taxi, please?

Würden Sie mir bitte ein Taxi bestellen?

vuerden zee meer bitter ain tarksi beshtellen?

Is there any mail for me?

Ist Post für mich da?

ist posst fuer mikh dar?

Sie können sich selbst einen Platz aussuchen.	You can pick your own site.
Sie bekommen einen Platz zugewiesen.	You'll be allocated a site.
Dies ist Ihre Platznummer.	This is your site number.
Kleben Sie dies bitte auf Ihr Auto.	Stick this on your car, please.
Sie dürfen diese Karte nicht verlieren.	Please don't lose this card.

7.2 Camping

Where's the manager?	Wo ist der Verwalter?
	vo ist der fairvalter?
Are we allowed to camp here?	Dürfen wir hier campen?
	duerfen veer heer kampen?
There are...of us and...tents	Wir sind...Personen und haben...Zelte
	veer zint ...perzoanen oont harben ...tselter
Can we pick our own place?	Dürfen wir selbst einen Platz aussuchen?
	duerfen veer zelpst ainen plats owszookhen?
Do you have a quiet spot for us?	Haben Sie einen ruhigen Platz für uns?
	harben zee ainen roohigen plats fuer oons?
Do you have any other pitches available?	Haben Sie keinen anderen freien Platz?
	harben zee kainen anderen fraien plats?
It's too windy/sunny/ shady here.	Hier ist zuviel Wind/Sonne/Schatten
	heer ist tsoofeel vint/zonner/shatten
It's too crowded here.	Hier ist es zu voll.
	heer ist es tsoo foll
The ground's too hard/uneven	Der Boden ist zu hart/ungleichmässig
	der boaden ist tsoo hart/oon-glaikh mayssikh

Do you have a level spot for the camper/caravan/folding caravan?	Haben Sie einen horizontalen Platz für das Wohnmobil/den Wohnwagen/Faltwagen?	*harben zee ainen horitsontarlen plats fuer dass voan-moabeel/dayn voanvargen/faltvargen?*
Could we have adjoining pitches?	Können wir beieinander stehen?	*koennen veer baiainander shtayhen?*
Can we park the car next to the tent?	Darf das Auto beim Zelt geparkt werden?	*darf dass owto baim tselt geparkt verden?*
How much is it per person/tent/caravan/car?	Was kostet es pro Person/Zelt/Wohnwagen/Auto?	*vass kostet ez pro perzoan/tselt/voanvargen/owto?*

Camping equipment

luggage space	das Gepäckapsis	*dass gepekapsis*
can opener	der Dosenöffner	*dayr doazen-oefner*
butane gas bottle	die Butangasflasche	*dee bootarn-gasflasher*
pannier	die Packtasche	*dee pakktasher*
gas cooker	der Gaskocher	*dayr gasskokher*
groundsheet	die Bodenplane	*dee boadenplarner*
mallet	der Hammer	*dayr hammer*
hammock	die Hängematte	*dee hengermatter*
jerry can	der Kanister	*dayr kannister*
campfire	das Lagerfeuer	*dass largerfoyer*
folding chair	der Klappstuhl	*dayr klapshtool*
insulated picnic box	die Kühltasche	*dee kuehltasher*
ice pack	das Kühlelemenz	*dass kuehlelement*

compass	der Kompass	dayr kompas
wick	der Glühstrumpf	dayr glueh-shtroompf
corkscrew	der Korkenzieher	dayr korkentseeyer
airbed	die Luftmatratze	dee looftmatrattser
airbed plug pump	der Matratzenstöpsel	dayr matrattsenshtoepse
awning	das Vordach	dass fordakh
karimat	die Matte	dee matter
pan	die Pfanne	dee pfanner
pan handle	der Pfannenstiel	dayr pfannen-shteel
primus stove	der Petroleumkocher	dayr petroaleyoomkokher
zip	der Reissverschluss	dayr raissfershluss
backpack	der Rucksack	dayr rookzakk
guy rope	die Zeltleine	dee tseltlainer
sleeping bag	der Schlafsack	dayr shlarfzak
storm lantern	die Sturmlaterne	dee shtoormlaterner
camp bed	die Liege	dee leeger
table	der Tisch	dayr tish
tent	das Zelt	dass tselt
tent peg	der Hering	dayr hayring
tent pole	die Zeltstange	dee tseltshtanger
vacuum flask	die Thermosflasche	dee termowsflasher
water bottle	die Feldflasche	dee feltflasher
clothes peg	die Wäscheklammer	dee vesherklummer
clothes line	die Wäscheleine	dee vesherlainer
windbreak	der Windschutz	dayr vintshoots
torch	die Taschenlampe	dee tashenlamper
pocket knife	das Taschenmesser	dass tashenmesser

Are there any...?	Gibt es...?
	gipt ez...?
– any hot showers?	Warmwasserduschen?
	varm vasser dooshen?
– washing machines?	Waschmaschinen?
	wash masheenen?
Is there a...on the site?	Gibt es auf dem Gelände...?
	gipt ez owf daym gelender...?
Is there a children's play area on the site?	...einen Kinderspielplatz?
	...ainen kinder-shpeel-plats?
Are there covered cooking facilities on the site?	...eine überdachte Kochgelegenheit?
	...ainer ueber-dakhter kokh-gelaygen hait?
Are we allowed to barbecue here?	Darf man hier grillen?
	darf man heer grillen?
Are there any power points?	Gibt es Elektroanschlüsse?
	gipt ez elektro-anshluesser?
When's the rubbish collected?	Wann wird der Abfall abgeholt?
	vann virt dayr apfal apgeholt?
Do you sell gas bottles (butane gas/propane gas)?	Verkaufen Sie Gasflaschen (Butangas/ Propangas)?
	fairkowfen zee gassflashen (bootarn- gass/proparn-gass)?

7.3 Hotel/B&B/apartment/holiday house

Do you have a single/double room available?	Haben Sie ein Einzelzimmer/ Doppelzimmer frei?
	harben zee ain aintsel-tsimmer/doppel -tsimmer frai?
per person/per room	pro Person/pro Zimmer
	pro perzoan/pro tsimmer
Does that include breakfast/ lunch/dinner?	Ist das einschliesslich Frühstück/ Mittagessen/Abendessen?
	ist dass ainshleeslikh frueh-shtuek/ mittark-essen/arbent-essen?

Toilette und Dusche sind
auf derselben Etage/in
Ihrem Zimmer.
Hier entlang bitte
Ihr Zimmer ist im...Stock, die
Nummer ist...

You can find the toilet and
shower on the same floor/en
suite.
This way, please.
Your room is on the...floor,
number...

Could we have two
adjoining rooms?

Können wir zwei Zimmer nebeneinander
bekommen?
*koennen veer tsvai tsimmer nayben-
ainander bekommen?*

with/without toilet/
bath/shower

mit/ohne eigener Toilette/eigenem Bad/
eigener Dusche
*mit/oaner aigener twaletter/aigenem
bart/aigener doosher*

(not) facing the street

(nicht) an der Strassenseite
(nikht) an dayr shtrassen-zaiter

with/without a view of the sea

mit/ohne Seesicht
mit/oaner zayzikht

Is there...in the hotel?

Gibt es im Hotel...?
gipt ez im hotel...?

Is there a lift in the hotel?

Gibt es im Hotel einen Fahrstuhl?
gipt ez im hotel ainen fahrshtool?

Do you have room service?

Gibt es im Hotel Zimmerservice?
gipt ez im hotel tsimmer zairviss?

Could I see the room?

Könnte ich das Zimmer mal sehen?
koennter ikh dass tsimmer marl zayhen?

I'll take this room.

Ich nehme dieses Zimmer.
ikh naymer deezes tsimmer

We don't like this one.

Dieses gefällt uns nicht.
deezes gefellt oons nikht

Do you have a larger/less expensive room?

Haben Sie ein grösseres/billigeres Zimmer?

harben zee ain groesseres/billeegeres tsimmer?

Could you put in a cot?

Können Sie ein Kinderbett dazustellen?

koennen zee ain kinder bet datsoo shtellen?

What time's breakfast?

Ab wann gibt es Frühstück?

ap vann gipt ez frueh-shtuek?

Where's the dining room?

Wo ist der Speisesaal?

vo ist dayr shpaize-zarl?

Can I have breakfast in my room?

Kann ich Frühstück aufs Zimmer bekommen?

kann ikh frueh-shtuek owfs tsimmer bekommen?

Where's the emergency exit/fire escape?

Wo ist der Notausgang/die Feuertreppe?

vo ist der noat-owsgang/dee foyer-trepper?

Where can I park my car (safely)?

Wo kann ich mein Auto (sicher) abstellen?

vo kann ikh main owto (zikher) apshtellen?

The key to room..., please.

Den Schlüssel für Zimmer...bitte.

dayn shluessel fuer tsimmer...bitter

Could you put this in the safe, please?

Darf ich dies bitte in Ihren Safe legen?

darf ikh dees bitter in eeren safe laygen?

Could you wake me at...tomorrow?

Wecken Sie mich morgen bitte um...Uhr?

vekken zee mikh morgen bitter oom... ooer?

Could you find a babysitter for me?

Können Sie mir einen Babysitter besorgen?

koennen zee meer ainen babysitter bezorgen?

Could I have an .. extra blanket/pillow?

Würden Sie bitte eine extra Decke Kissen bringen?

vuerden zee bitter ainer ekstrar dekker/ kissen bringen?

When are the sheets/towels/ tea towels changed?	Wann werden die Bettlaken/Handtücher/ Geschirrtücher gewechselt?
	vann verden dee bett larken/hant tuekher/geshirr tuekher gevekhselt?

7.4 Complaints

We can't sleep because it is too noisy.	Wir können durch den Lärm nicht schlafen.
	veer koennen doorkh den lerm nikht shlarfen
Could you turn the radio down, please?	Könnten Sie das Radio bitte etwas leiser stellen?
	koennten zee dass radeeo bitter etvass laizer shtellen?
We're out of toilet paper.	Das Toilettenpapier ist alle.
	dass twaletten-papeer ist aller
There aren't any.../ there's not enough...	Es gibt keine.../nicht genug...
	es gipt kainer.../nikht genook...
The bed linen's dirty.	Die Bettwäsche ist schmutzig.
	dee bettvesher ist shmootsikh
The room hasn't been cleaned.	Das Zimmer ist nicht saubergemacht.
	dass tsimmer ist nikht zowber gemakht
The kitchen is not clean.	Die Küche ist nicht sauber.
	dee kuekher ist nikht zowber
The kitchen utensils are dirty.	Die Küchengeräte sind schmutzig.
	dee kuekhen gerayter zint shmootsikh
The heater's not working.	Die Heizung funktioniert nicht.
	dee haitsoong foonk tseeoneert nikht
There's no (hot) water/electricity.	Es gibt kein (warmes) Wasser/keinen Strom.
	ez gipt kain (varmez) vasser/kainen shtroam
...is broken	... ist kaputt
	...ist kapoott

Could you have that seen to? | Können Sie das in Ordnung bringen lassen?
koennen zee dass in ordnoong bringen lassen?

Could I have another room/site? | Könnte ich ein anderes Zimmer/einen anderen Stellplatz bekommen?
koennter ikh ain underes tsimmer/ainen anderen stellplats bekommen?

The bed creaks terribly. | Das Bett knarrt furchtbar.
dass bet knarrt foorkhtbar

The bed sags. | Das Bett biegt sich durch.
dass bet beekt zikh doorkh

Could we have a board to put underneath? | Haben Sie ein Brett zum Drunterlegen?
harben zee ain bret tsoom droonter laygen?

It's too noisy. | Es ist zu laut.
ez ist tsoo lowt

We have trouble with bugs/insects. | Wir haben Ärger mit Ungeziefer/Insekten.
veer harben airger mit oongetseefer/ inzekten

This place is full of mosquitos. | Es wimmelt hier von Mücken.
ez vimmelt heer fon mueken

– cockroaches | Es wimmelt hier von Kakerlaken.
ez vimmelt heer fon karker larken

7.5 Departure

See also **8.2 Settling the bill**

I'm leaving tomorrow. Could I settle my bill, please?	Ich reise morgen ab. Könnte ich jetzt bitte abrechnen? *ikh raizer morgen ap. koennter ikh yetst bitter aprekhnen?*
What time should we vacate?	Wann müssen wir den/das/die... verlassen? *vann muessen veer dayn/dass/dee... fairlassen?*
Could I have my passport back, please?	Würden Sie mir bitte die Kaution/den Pass wiedergeben? *vuerden zee meer bitter dee kowtseeoan/dayn pass veeder-gayben?*
We're in a terrible hurry.	Wir haben grosse Eile. *veer harben groasser ailer*
Could we leave our luggage here until we leave?	Dürfen wir unsere Koffer bis zur Abreise hier stehenlassen? *duerfen veer oonzere koffer biss tsoor apraizer heer shtayen lassen?*
Thanks for your hospitality.	Vielen Dank für die Gastlichkeit/die Gastfreundschaft. *feelen dunk fuer dee gastlikh kait/dee gast-froynt-shaft*

8. Money matters

● In general, banks are open to the public between 9am and 4.30pm. Some types of bank, smaller outlets and banks in smaller towns and villages often close for lunch between 12 noon and 2pm. Banks are closed on a Saturday. The sign *Geld/wechsel/ausländische Währung* indicates that money can be changed.

8.1 Banks

Where can I find a bank/an exchange office around here?	Wo ist hier eine Bank/eine Wechselstube?
	vo ist heer ainer bank/ainer vekhsel-shtoober?
Where can I find a cash point/ATM?	Wo finde ich einen Geldautomaten?
	vo finder ish ainen geldowtomarten?
Where can I cash this traveller's cheque?	Wo kann ich diesen Reisescheck einlösen?
	vo kann ikh deezen raizer shekk/postbar shekk ainloezen?
Can I cash this...here?	Kann ich hier diesen...einlösen?
	kann ikh heer deezen...ainloezen?
Can I withdraw money on my credit card here?	Kann ich hier mit einer Kreditkarte Geld bekommen?
	kann ikh heer mit ainer kredit-karter gelt bekommen?
What's the minimum/maximum amount?	Was ist das Minimum/Maximum?
	vass ist dass minimoom/maksimoom?
Can I take out less than that?	Darf ich auch weniger abheben?
	darf ikh owkh vayniger aphayben?
I've had some money transferred here. Has it arrived yet?	Ich habe Geld überweisen lassen. Ist es schon eingegangen?
	ikh harber gelt ueber vaizen lassen. ist ez shoan ain gegangen?
These are the details of my bank in the UK.	Dies sind die Angaben von meiner Bank in England.
	deez zint dee angarben fon mainer bank in englant

This is my bank account number.	Dies ist meine Kontonummer.
	deez ist mainer konto-noomer
I'd like to change some money.	Ich möchte Geld wechseln.
	ikh moekhter gelt vekhseln
– pounds into...	– (englische) Pfund in...
	– (englisher) pfoont in...
– dollars into...	– Dollars in... *– dollars in...*
– Euros into...	Euro in... *oiro in...*
What's the exchange rate?	Wie hoch ist der Wechselkurs?
	vee hokh ist dayr vekhsel koors?
Could you give me some small change with it?	Können Sie mir auch etwas Kleingeld geben?
	koennen zee meer owkh etvass klaingelt gayben?
This is not right.	Das stimmt nicht.
	dass shtimmt nikht

8.2 Settling the bill

Unterschreiben Sie bitte hier.	Sign here, please.
Sie müssen dies ausfüllen.	Fill this out, please.
Darf ich bitte Ihren Pass haben?	Could I have your passport?
Darf ich Ihren Ausweis sehen?	Could I see some identification, please?

Could you put it on my bill?	Könnten Sie das auf die Rechnung setzen?
	koennten zee dass owf dee rekhnoong setsen?
Does this amount include service?	Ist die Bedienung in diesem Betrag enthalten?
	ist dee bedeenoong in deezem betrark enthalten?

Can I pay by...?	Kann ich mit...bezahlen?
	kann ikh mit...betsarlen?
Can I pay by credit card?	Kann ich mit (einer) Kreditkarte bezahlen?
	kann ikh mit (ainer) kredit karter betsarlen?
Can I pay by traveller's cheque?	Kann ich mit einem Reisescheck bezahlen?
	kann ikh mit ainem raizer shekk betsarlen?
Can I pay with foreign currency?	Kann ich in ausländischer Währung bezahlen?
	kann ikh in owslendisher vayroong betsarlen?
You've given me too much/ you haven't given me enough change.	Sie haben mir zuviel/zuwenig (wieder) gegeben.
	zee harben meer tsoofeel/tsoovaynikh (veeder) gegayben
Could you check this again, please?	Würden Sie das noch mal nachrechnen?
	vuerden zee dass nokh marl nakh-rekhnen?
Could I have a receipt, please?	Ich hätte gern eine Quittung/den Kassenzettel?
	ikh hetter gayrn ainer kvittoong/dayn kassen tsettel?
I don't have enough money on me.	Ich habe nicht genug Geld bei mir.
	ikh harber nikht genook gelt bai meer
This is for you.	Bitte, das ist für Sie.
	bitter, dass ist fuer zee
Keep the change.	Behalten Sie das Wechselgeld.
	beharlten zee dass vekhselgelt

Wir nehmen keine Kreditkarten/ Reiseschecks/Auslands währungen an	We don't accept credit cards/ traveller's cheques/foreign currency
Nur Barzahlung	Cash only

9. Communications

9.1 Post

● Post offices are open from Monday to Friday between 8.30am and 5pm. In smaller towns the post office closes at lunch. On Saturdays they are open until 12 noon. Stamps are only available at post offices and some hotel receptions. Post boxes are yellow.

Briefmarken	Päckchen/Pakete	Postanweisung
stamps	parcels	money orders

Where's...?	Wo ist...?
	vo ist...?
Where's the post office?	Wo ist hier ein Postamt?
	vo ist heer ain postamt?
Where's the main post office?	Wo ist die Hauptpost?
	vo ist dee howptpost?
Where's the postbox?	Wo ist hier ein Briefkasten?
	vo ist heer ain breefkasten?
Which counter should I go to...?	An welchem Schalter kann ich... ?
	an velkhem shalter kann ikh...?
Poste restante	Postlagernd
	postlargernt
Is there any mail for me? My name's…	Ist Post für mich da? Mein Name ist...
	ist post fuer mikh dar? main narmer ist...
Can I make photocopies/ send a fax here?	Kann ich hier fotokopieren/telefaxen?
	kann ikh heer foto kopeeren/telefaksen?
How much is that per page?	Wieviel kostet das pro Seite?
	veefeel kostet dass pro zaiter?

Stamps

What's the postage for a...to...?	Wieviel muss auf einen/ein(e)...nach...?
	veefeel mooss owf ainen/ain(er)... nakh...?
Are there enough stamps on it?	Sind genug Briefmarken drauf?
	zint genook breefmarken drowf?

I'd like...stamps to...	Ich möchte...Briefmarken zu...
	ikh moekhter...breefmarken tsoo...
I'd like to send this...	Ich möchte dies...schicken.
	ikh moekhter dees...shikken
– express.	Ich möchte dies per Eilboten schicken.
	ikh moekhter dees payr ailboaten shikker
– by air mail.	Ich möchte dies per Luftpost schicken.
	ikh moekhter dees payr looftpost shikker
– by registered mail.	Ich möchte dies per Einschreiben schicken.
	ikh moekhter dees payr ainshraiben shikken

9.2 Telephone

See also **1.8 Telephone alphabet**

● All phone booths offer a direct international service to the UK. To phone the UK dial 0044, plus the UK area code without the first 0. They are either coin phones or card phones. The cards can be bought at post offices. Some telephone booths will also accept credit cards. Phone booths do not accept incoming calls. A reverse-charge call (*ein R-Gespräch*) has to go via the operator. When phoning someone in Germany, you may be greeted with the subscriber's name or with *Hallo* or *Ja*.

Is there a phone box around here?	Ist hier eine Telefonzelle in der Nähe?
	ist heer ainer telefoan-tseller in dayr nayher?
Could I use your phone, please?	Dürfte ich Ihr Telefon benutzen?
	duerfter ikh eer telefoan benuetsen?
Do you have a (city/region)... phone directory?	Haben Sie ein Telefonbuch (von der Stadt.../dem Bezirk...)?
	harben zee ain telefoan-bookh (fon dayr shtat.../daym betseerk...)?

Where can I get a phone card?	Wo kann ich eine Telefonkarte kaufen?
	vo kann ikh ainer telefoan-karter kowfen?
Could you give me...?	Könnten Sie mir...geben?
	koennten zee meer...gayben?
– the number for international directory enquiries	Könnten Sie mir die Nummer der Auslandsauskunft geben?
	koennten zee meer dee noomer dayr owslants-owskoonft gayben?
– the number of room...	Könnten Sie mir die Nummer von Zimmer ...geben?
	koennten zee meer dee noomer fon tsimmer ...gayben?
– the international access code	Könnten Sie mir die internationale Nummer geben?
	koennten zee meer dee inter-natseeo-narle noommer gayben?
– the country code for...	Könnten Sie mir die Ländervorwahl von ... geben?
	koennten zee meer dee lender forvarl fon ...gayben?
– the trunk code for...	Könnten Sie mir die Vorwahl von... geben?
	koennten zee meer dee forvarl fon ...gayben?
– the number of...	Könnten Sie mir die Rufnummer von ... geben?
	koennten zee meer dee roofnoomer fon ...gayben?
Could you check if this this number's correct?	Könnten Sie kontrollieren, ob diese Nummer richtig ist?
	koennten zee kontroleeren, op deezer noomer rikhtikh ist?
Can I dial international direct?	Kann ich automatisch ins Ausland telefonieren?
	kan ikh owtomatish ins owslant telefoaneeren?

Do I have to go through the switchboard?	Muss ich über die Telefonistin telefonieren?
	mooss ikh ueber dee telefoanisstin telefoaneeren?
Do I have to dial '0' first?	Muss ich erst eine Null wählen?
	mooss ikh erst ainer nool vaylen?
Do I have to book my calls?	Muss ich ein Gespräch anmelden?
	mooss ikh ain geshprekh anmelden?
Could you dial this number for me, please?	Würden Sie bitte folgende Nummer für mich anrufen?
	vuerden zee bitter folgender noommer fuer mikh anroofen?
Could you put me through to.../ extension..., please?	Verbinden Sie mich bitte mit.../Apparat...
	fairbinden zee mikh bitter mit.../ apparart...
I'd like to place a reverse-charge call to…	Ich möchte ein R-Gespräch mit...
	ikh moekhter ain air-geshprekh mit...
What's the charge per minute?	Wieviel kostet das pro Minute?
	veefeel kostet dass pro meenooter?
Have there been any calls for me?	Hat jemand für mich angerufen?
	hat yaymant fuer mikh angeroofen?

The conversation

Hello, this is...	Guten Tag, ... hier
	gooten tark, ... heer
Who is this, please?	Mit wem spreche ich?
	mit vaym shprekher ikh?
Is this...?	Spreche ich mit...?
	shprekher ikh mit...?
I'm sorry, I've dialled the wrong number.	Entschuldigung, ich habe mich verwählt.
	ent shool digung, ikh harber mikh fairvaylt
I can't hear you	Ich kann Sie nicht verstehen
	ikh kann zee nikht fairshtayhen
I'd like to speak to...	Ich möchte...sprechen

| | *ikh moekhter...shprekhen* |

Extension...please	Apparat...bitte
	apparart ...bitter
Could you ask him/her to call me back?	Er/sie möchte mich bitte zurückrufen
	ayr/zee moekhter mikh bitter tsooruekh-roofen
My name's... My number's...	Mein Name ist... Meine Nummer ist...
	main narmer ist... mainer noommer ist...
'll call back tomorrow.	Ich rufe ihn/sie morgen wieder an.
	ikh roofer een/zee morgen veeder an

Telefon für Sie.	There's a phone call for you.
Sie müssen erst eine Null wählen.	You have to dial '0' first.
(Einen) Augenblick bitte.	One moment, please.
Es antwortet niemand.	There's no answer.
Die Nummer ist besetzt.	The line's engaged.
Wollen Sie warten?.	Do you want to hold?
Ich verbinde.	Putting you through.
Sie haben die falsche Nummer (gewählt).	You've got a wrong number.
Er/sie ist im Augenblick nicht da/im Haus.	He's/she's not here right now.
Er/sie ist...wieder zu erreichen.	He'll/she'll be back...
Dies ist der Anrufbeantworter von...	This is the answering machine of...

9.3 Email and internet

Can I use the internet/check my emails here?	Kann ich das Internet hier benutzen /meine E-Mails abrufen?
	kunn ish dars intairnet heer benootsen/ maine eemails abroofen?
Do you have (free) WiFi?	Haben Sie (kostenloses) WLAN?
	harben zee (kostenloazes) vlarn?
Where can I find an internet café?	Wo finde ich ein Internetcafé?
	vo finder ish ain intairnetkarfay?
How much does the internet per hour?	Wie viel kostet das Internet pro Stunde?
	vee feel kostet dars intairnet proa shtoonder?
Can I connect my computer laptop here?	Kann ich meinen Computer/Laptop hier anschließen?
	kunn ish mainen kompyootair/ leptop heer unshlisen?
What is the password?	Wie ist das Passwort?
	vee ist dars pusswoart?
Can I use a printer?	Kann ich den Drucker benutzen?
	kunn ish dayn drookker benootsen?
Are you on Facebook?	Bist du bei Facebook?
	bist doo bai faysbook?
Can I add you as a friend?	Kann ich dich als Freund hinzufügen?
	kunn ish dish als froynd hintsoofuegen?
Are you on Twitter?	Bist du bei Twitter?
	bist doo bai tvitter?
What is your username?	Wie ist dein Benutzername?
	vee ist dain benootsairnarme?
My email address is…	Meine E-Mail Adresse ist...
	maine eemail ardresser ist...
What is your email address?	Wie ist deine E-Mail Adresse?
	vee ist daine eemail ardresser?

10. Shopping

● Opening times: Supermarkets and department stores are open
Monday to Friday 8.30/9am–5.30/6pm, on Saturdays they are usually
closed after 2pm. However, every first Saturday of the month is a *langer
Samstag* (long Saturday) which means that shops stay open until about
6pm. In many larger towns shops stay open until 8.30pm on a Thursday.
Smaller shops may close for lunch between 12 noon and 2pm and on
Wednesday afternoons.

10.1 Shopping conversations

Where can I get...?	In welchem Geschäft kann ich... bekommen?
	in velkhem gesheft kan ikh... bekommen?
When does this shop open?	Wann hat dieses Geschäft geöffnet?
	van hat deezez gesheft geoeffnet?
Could you tell me where the... department is?	Können Sie mir sagen, wo die... Abteilung ist?
	koennen zee meer zargen vo dee... aptailoong ist?
Could you help me, please? I'm looking for...	Können Sie mir bitte helfen? Ich suche...
	koennen zee meer bitter helfen? ikh zookher...
Do you sell English/American newspapers?	Verkaufen Sie englische/amerikanische Zeitungen?
	fairkowfen zee englisher/amerikarnisher tsai-toongen?
No, I'd like...	Nein, ich möchte...
	nain, ikh moekhter...

🖢

Werden Sie schon bedient?   Are you being served?

Andenkenladen	souvenir shop
Antiquitäten	antiques
Bäckerei	bakery
Beleuchtung	lighting
Buchhandlung	bookshop
Drogerie	chemist
Einkaufszentrum	shopping centre
Eisenwarengeschäft	hardware store
Elektrogeräte	electrical appliances
Fahrradgeschäft	cycle shop
Feinkost	delicatessen
Fischgeschäft	fishmonger
Flohmarkt	fleamarket
Florist	florist
Frisör	hairdresser
Gärtnerei	nursery
Geschäft	shop
Getränkemarkt	drinks store
Handarbeitsgeschäft	needlework and wool shop
Handlung	dealer
Haushaltswaren	household goods
Heimwerker Markt	DIY-store
Kaufhaus	department store
Konditorei	cake shop
Kosmetiksalon	beauty parlour
Kürschner	furrier
Kurzwarenhandlung	haberdashery
Laden	shop
Metzgerei	butcher's
Molkereigeschäft	dairy
Münzwäscherei	laundrette
Musikalienhandlung	music shop
Obst und Gemüse	greengrocer
Ökoladen	health food shop
Optiker	opticians
Pelze	fur
Rauchwarengeschäft	tobacconist
Raumausstattung(shaus)	interior decorator
Reinigung	dry cleaner
Musikgeschäft	record shop
Schlachter	butcher
Schmuck	jeweller
Schuhgeschäft	shoe shop
Schuhmacher/ Schuster	cobbler
Spielzeuggeschäft	toy shop
Spirituosenhandlung	off licence
Sportartikel	sports shop
Supermarkt	supermarket
Süsswaren	sweet shop
Tante-Emma-Laden	corner shop
Trafik	tobacconist
Uhrengeschäft	clock shop/jeweller
Wäscherei	laundry
Zoohandlung	pet shop

Sonst noch (et)was?	Anything else?

I'm just looking,
if that's all right
Ich möchte mich nur mal umsehen
ikh moekhter mikh noor marl oom zayhen

Yes, I'd also like...
Ja, bitte auch noch...
yar, bitter owkh nokh...

No, thank you. That's all.
Nein, danke. Das ist alles.
nain, dunker. dass ist alles

Could you show me...?
Können Sie mir...zeigen?
koennen zee meer...tsaigen?

I'd prefer...
Ich möchte lieber...
ikh moekhter leeber...

This is not what I'm looking for
Das ist nicht, was ich suche
dass ist nikht vass ikh zookher

Thank you. I'll keep looking.
Ich sehe mich erst noch mal weiter um.
ikh zayher mikh airst nokh marl vaiter oom

Do you have something...?
Haben Sie nicht etwas, was...ist?
harben zee nikht etvass, vass...ist?

– less expensive?
Haben Sie nicht etwas Billigeres?
harben zee nikht etvass billigerez?

– something smaller?
Haben Sie nicht etwas Kleineres?
harben zee nikht etvass klainerez?

– something larger?
Haben Sie nicht etwas Grösseres?
harben zee nikht etvass groerserez?

I'll take this one.
Ich nehme dies.
ikh naymer deez

Does it come with
instructions?
Ist eine Gebrauchsanweisung dabei?
ist ainer gebrowkhs-anvai-zoong darbai?

It's too expensive.
Ich finde es zu teuer.
ikh finder ez tsoo toyer

I'll give you...
Ich biete Ihnen...
ikh beeter eenen...

Could you keep this for me? I'll come back for it later.	Kann ich ihn/sie/es hierlassen? Ich hole ihn/sie/es nachher ab.
	kan ikh een/zee/es heerlassen? ikh hoaler een/zee/es nakhherr ap
Have you got a bag for me, please?	Haben Sie bitte eine Tüte für mich?
	harben zee bitter ainer tueter fuer mikh?
Could you giftwrap it, please?	Könnten Sie es bitte in Geschenkpapier einpacken?
	koennten zee ez bitter in geshenk-papeer ainpakken?

(Es) tut mir leid, das haben/ führen wir nicht.	I'm sorry, we don't have that.
(Es) tut mir leid, das ist ausverkauft.	I'm sorry, we're sold out.
Tut mir leid, das kriegen wir erst...wieder rein.	I'm sorry, that won't be in until...
Sie können an der Kasse zahlen.	You can pay at the cash desk.
Wir nehmen keine Kreditkarten an.	We don't accept credit cards.
Wir nehmen keine Reiseschecks an.	We don't accept traveller's cheques.
Wir nehmen kein ausländisches Geld/keine Fremdwährungen an.	We don't accept foreign currency.

10.2 Food

I'd like a hundred grams of..., please.	Hundert Gramm...bitte.
	hoondert gramm...bitter
– five hundred grams/half a kilo of…	Fünfhundert Gramm/ein halbes Kilo...bitte
	fuenfhoondert gramm/ain halbes keelo...bitter

– a kilo of...	Ein Kilo...bitte	*ain keelo...bitter*
Could you...it for me, please?	Würden Sie es mir bitte...?	
		vuerden zee es meer bitter...?
Could you slice it/dice it for me, please?	Würden Sie es mir bitte in Scheiben/Stücke/(kleine)Würfel schneiden?	
		vuerden zee es meer bitter in shaiben/shtueker/(klainer) vuerfel shnaiden?
Could you grate it for me, please?	Würden Sie es mir bitte reiben?	
		vuerden zee es meer bitter raiben?
Can I order it?	Kann ich es bestellen?	
		kan ikh es beshtellen?
I'll pick it up tomorrow/at...	Ich hole es morgen/um...Uhr ab.	
		ikh hoaler es morgen/oom...oor ap
Can you eat/drink this?	Kann man das essen/trinken?	
		kan man dass essen/trinken?
What's in it?	Woraus besteht es?	
		vorows beshtayt es?

10.3 Clothing and shoes

I saw something in the window. Shall I point it out?	Ich habe im Schaufenster etwas gesehen. Soll ich es Ihnen zeigen?	
		ikh harber im showfenster etvass gesayhen. zoll ikh ez eenen tsaigen?
I'd like something to go with this.	Ich möchte gern etwas, was hierzu passt.	
		ikh moekhter gayrn etvass, vass heertsoo passt
Do you have shoes to match this?	Haben Sie Schuhe in derselben Farbe wie diese hier?	
		harben zee shooer in derselben farber vee deezer heer?
I'm a size...in the UK.	In England habe ich Grösse...	
		in englant harber ikh groesser...
Can I try this on?	Darf ich dies anprobieren?	
		darf ikh dees anprobeeren?

Where's the fitting room?	Wo ist die Anprobe?
	vo ist dee anprober?
It doesn't fit.	Es passt mir nicht.
	es passt meer nikht
This is the right size.	Das ist die richtige Grösse.
	dass ist dee rikhtiger groesser
It doesn't suit me.	Es steht mir nicht.
	es shtayt meer nikht
Do you have this in...?	Haben Sie dies/diese auch in...?
	harben zee dees/deezer owkh in...?
The heel's too high/low.	Ich finde den Absatz zu hoch/niedrig.
	ikh finder den apzats tsoo hokh/needrikh
Is this/are these genuine leather?	Ist dies/sind diese aus echtem Leder?
	ist dees/zint deezer ows ekhtem layder?
I'm looking for a...for a... -year-old baby/child.	Ich suche ein(en)/eine...für ein Baby/Kind von...Jahren.
	ikh zookher ain(en)/ainer...fuer ain baby/kint fon...yahren
I'd like a...in...	Ich hätte gern ein(en)/eine...aus
	ikh hetter gayrn ain(en)/ainer...ows
– silk.	Ich hätte gern ein(en)/eine...aus Seide
	ikh hetter gayrn ain(en)/ainer... ows zaider
– cotton.	Ich hätte gern ein(en)/eine...aus Baumwolle
	ikh hetter gayrn ain(en)/ainer... ows bowmvoller
– woollen.	Ich hätte gern ein(en)/eine...aus Wolle
	ikh hetter gayrn ain(en)/ainer... ows voller

Chemisch reinigen	Maschinenwaschbar	Nicht bügeln
Dry clean	Machine washable	Do not iron
Handwäsche	Nass aufhängen	Nicht schleudern
Hand wash	Drip dry	Do not spin

– linen.	Ich hätte gern ein(en)/eine...aus Leinen
	ikh hetter gayrn ain(en)/ainer...
	ows lainen
What temperature can I wash it at?	Bei welcher Temperatur kann ich es waschen?
	bai velkher temperatoor kan ikh es vashen?
Will it shrink in the wash?	Läuft es (in der Wäsche) ein?
	loyft es (in der wesher) ain?

At the cobbler

Could you mend these shoes?	Können Sie diese Schuhe reparieren?
	koennen zee deezer shooer repareeren?
Could you put new soles/heels on these?	Können Sie diese hier versohlen/die Absätze erneuern?
	koennen zee deezer heer fairzoalen/dee apsetzer ernoyern?
When will they be ready?	Wann sind sie fertig?
	vann zint zee fairtikh?
I'd like..., please.	Ich möchte (gern)...
	ikh moekhter (gayrn)...
– a tin of shoe polish.	Ich möchte gern eine Dose Schuhcreme.
	ikh moekhter gayrn ainer doazer shookremer
– a pair of shoelaces.	Ich möchte gern ein Paar Schuhbänder.
	ikh moekhter gayrn ain par shoobender

10.4 Photographs: digital and film

I'd like a film for this camera, please.

Ich möchte einen Film für diesen Apparat.

ikh moekhter ainen film fuer deezen apparart

I need a memory card /charger/battery for my digital camera.

Ich brauche eine Speicherkarte/ Aufladegerät/Batterie für meine Digitalkamera.

ish browkhe aine shpaishairkarter/ owflardegerayt/ bateree fuer maine digitarlkumerar.

Where can I have a passport photo taken?

Wo kann ich ein Passbild machen lassen?

vo kan ikh ain passbilt makhen lassen?

Problems

Could you have a look at my camera, please? It's not working

Könnten Sie sich bitte mal die Kamera ansehen? Sie funktioniert nicht mehr

koennten zee zikh bitter marl dee kamerar anzayhen? zee foonk tseeoneert nikht mair

Should I replace the batteries?

Muss ich die Batterien auswechseln?

mooss ikh dee battereeyen ows vekhseln?

The...is broken.

Der/die/das...ist kaputt.

dayr/dee/dass...ist kapoott

The film's jammed.

Der Film klemmt.

dayr film klemmt

The flash isn't working.

Das Blitzlicht funktioniert nicht.

dass blits likht foonk tseeoneert nikht

Processing and prints

I'd like to have this film developed/printed, please.	Ich möchte diesen Film entwickeln/ abziehen lassen.
	ikh moekhter deezen film entvikkeln/ap tseeyen lassen
Can I print digital photos here?	Kann ich hier digitale Fotos ausdrucken?
	kunn ish heer digitarle foatos owsdrookken?
glossy/mat	glänzend/matt
	glentsent/mat
7 x 5	Sieben mal fünf
	zeeben marl fuenf
I'd like to re-order these photos.	Ich möchte diese Fotos nachbestellen.
	ikh moekhter deezer fotos nakh beshtellen
I'd like to have this photo enlarged.	Ich möchte dieses Foto vergrössern lassen.
	ikh moekhter deezez foto fair groessern lassen
What sizes are available?	Zwischen welchen Größen kann ich wählen?
	tsvishen velshen groesen kunn ish waylen?
How much does it cost per image?	Wie viel kostet es pro Bild?
	vee feel kostet es proa bilt?
How much is processing?	Wieviel kostet das Entwickeln?
	veefeel kostet dass entvikkeln?
– printing	Wieviel kosten die Abzüge?
	veefeel kosten dee aptsueger?
– to re-order	Wieviel kostet die Nachbestellung?
	veefeel kostet dee nakh beshtelloong?
– the enlargement	Wieviel kostet die Vergrösserung?
	veefeel kostet dee fair groesseroong?
When will they be ready?	Wann sind sie fertig?
	vann zint zee fairtikh?

| Can you put my photos on a CD? | Können Sie meine Fotos auf eine CD machen? |
| | *koennen zee maine foatos owf aine tsede markhen?* |

Welchen Schnitt möchten Sie?	How do you want it cut?
Welches Modell möchten Sie?	What style did you have in mind?
Welche Farbe soll es sein?	What colour did you want it?
Ist das die richtige Temperatur?	Is the temperature all right for you?
Wünschen Sie etwas zu(m) Lesen?	Would you like something to read?
Wünschen Sie etwas zu trinken?	Would you like a drink?
Ist es so richtig?	Is this what you had in mind?

10.5 At the hairdresser's

Do I have to make an appointment?	Muss ich einen Termin machen?
	mooss ikh ainen termeen makhen?
Can I come in straight away?	Kann ich sofort drankommen?
	kann ikh zofort drannkommen?
How long will I have to wait?	Wie lange muss ich warten?
	vee langer mooss ikh varten?
I'd like a shampoo/haircut.	Ich möchte mir die Haare waschen/ schneiden lassen.
	ikh moekhter meer dee haarer vashen/ shnaiden lassen
Do you have a colour chart, please?	Hätten Sie eine Farbenkarte?
	hetten zee ainer farben karter?
I want to keep it the same colour.	Ich möchte die Farbe behalten.
	ikh moekhter dee farber behalten

I'd like it darker/lighter.	Ich möchte es dunkler/heller haben.
	ikh moekhter ez doonkler/heller harben
I'd like/I don't want hairspray.	Ich möchte (keinen) Haarfestiger.
	ikh moekhter (kainen) haarfestigger
– gel.	Ich möchte (kein) Gel.
	ikh moekhter (kain) jell
– lotion.	Ich möchte (keine) Lotion.
	ikh moekhter (kainer) loatseeyoan
I'd like a short fringe.	Ich möchte meinen Pony kurz tragen.
	ikh moekhter mainen pony koorts tragen
Not too short at the back.	Hinten nicht zu kurz schneiden bitte.
	hinten nikht tsoo koorts shnaiden bitter
Not too long here.	Hier bitte nicht zu lang.
	heer bitter nikht tsoo lang
I'd like a facial.	Ich möchte eine Gesichtsmaske.
	ikh moekhter ainer gezikhts-masker
– a manicure.	Ich möchte mich maniküren lassen.
	ikh moekhter mikh manni-kueren lassen
– a massage.	Ich möchte eine Massage.
	ikh moekhter ainer massarjer
Could you trim my fringe?	Würden Sie mir bitte den Pony kürzen?
	vuerden zee meer bitter dayn pony kuertsen?
– my beard?/my moustache?	Würden Sie mir bitte den Bart/Schnurrbart stutzen?
	vuerden zee meer bitter dayn bart/shnoorbart shtootsen?
I'd like a shave, please.	Rasieren bitte.
	razeeren bitter
I'd like a wet shave, please.	Ich möchte bitte nass rasiert werden.
	ikh moekhter bitter nass razeert verden

11. At the Tourist Information Centre

11.1 Places of interest

Where's the Tourist Information, please?	Wo ist der Fremdenverkehrsverein?
	vo ist dayr fremden-fayr-kayrs-fairrain?
Do you have a city map?	Haben Sie einen Stadtplan?
	harben zee ainen shtatplan?
Could you give me some information about...?	Können Sie mir Auskunft geben über...?
	koennen zee meer owskoonft gayben ueber...?
How much is that?	Wieviel kostet das?
	veefeel kostet dass?
What are the main places of interest?	Welches sind die wichtigsten Sehenswürdigkeiten?
	velkhez zint dee vikhtikhsten zayhens-vuerdikh-kaiten?
Could you point them out on the map?	Könnten Sie mir die auf dem Plan zeigen?
	koennten zee meer dee owf daym plarn tsaigen?
What do you recommend?	Was empfehlen Sie uns?
	vass empfaylen zee oons?
We'll be here for a few hours.	Wir bleiben hier ein paar Stunden.
	veer blaiben heer ain par shtoonden
– a day.	Wir bleiben hier einen Tag.
	veer blaiben heer ainen tark
– a week.	Wir bleiben hier eine Woche.
	veer blaiben heer ainer vokher
We're interested in...	Wir interessieren uns für...
	veer interesseeren oons fuer...
Is there a scenic walk around the city?	Können wir einen Stadtrundgang machen?
	koennen veer ainen shtat-roont-gang makhen?
How long does it take?	Wie lange dauert der?
	vee langer dowert dayr?

Where does it start/end?	Wo ist der Anfang/das Ende?
	vo ist der anfang/dass ender?
Are there any boat cruises here?	Gibt es hier Rundfahrtboote/-schiffe/ Ausflugsschiffe?
	gipt es heer roont-fahrt-boater/shiffer/ ows-flooks-shiffer?
Where can we board?	Wo können wir an Bord gehen?
	vo koennen veer an bort gayhen?
Are there any bus tours?	Gibt es Busrundfahrten?
	gipt es boos-roont-fahrten?
Where do we get on?	Wo müssen wir einsteigen?
	vo muessen veer ainshtaigen?
Is there a guide who speaks English?	Gibt es einen englisch sprechenden Führer?
	gipt ez ainen english shprekhenden fuerer?
Are there any excursions?	Gibt es Ausflüge?
	gipt ez owsflueger?
What trips can we take around the area?	Welche Ausflüge in die Umgebung kann man machen?
	velkher owsflooger in dee oom-gay-boong kann man makhen?
Where do they go to?	Wohin gehen die?
	vohin gayhen dee?
We'd like to go to...	Wir möchten nach...
	veer moekhten nakh...
How long is the trip?	Wie lange dauert der Ausflug?
	vee langer dowert dayr owsflook?
How long do we stay in...?	Wie lange bleiben wir in...?
	vee langer blaiben veer in...?
Are there any guided tours?	Gibt es Führungen?
	gipt ez fyueroongen?
How much free time will we have there?	Wieviel Freizeit haben wir da?
	veefeel fraitsait harben veer dar?
We want to go hiking.	Wir möchten eine Wanderung machen.
	veer moekhten ainer vanderoong makhen

Can we hire a guide?	Können wir einen Führer engagieren?
	koennen veer ainen fuerer engajeeren?
What time does...open/close?	Wann öffnet/schliesst (der/die/das)...?
	van oeffnet/shleest (dayr/dee/dass)...?
What days is...open/closed?	An welchen Tagen ist der/die/das... geöffnet/geschlossen?
	an velkhen targen ist dayr/dee/dass ... geoeffnet/geshlossen?
What's the admission price?	Wieviel kostet der Eintritt?
	veefeel kostet dayr aintrit?
Is there a group discount?	Gibt es Gruppenermässigung?
	gipt es groopen ermayssigoong?
Is there a child discount?	Gibt es Ermässigung für Kinder?
	gipt es ermayssigoong fuer kinder?
Is there a student discount?	Gibt es Studentenrabatt?
	gibt es shtoodentenrarbutt?
Is there a discount for pensioners?	Gibt es Ermässigung für Senioren?
	gipt es ermayssigoong fuer zeneeoren?
Can I take (flash) photos/ can I film here?	Darf ich hier (mit Blitzlicht) fotografieren/ filmen?
	darf ikh heer (mit blitslikht) foto-grafeeren/filmen?
Do you have any postcards of...?	Verkaufen Sie Ansichtskarten von dem/ der...?
	fayrkowfen zee an-sikhts-karten fon daym/ dayr...?
Do you have an English...?	Haben Sie ein(en)/eine...auf englisch?
	harben zee ain(en)/ainer...owf english?
– an English catalogue?	Haben Sie einen Katalog auf englisch?
	harben zee ainen kataloak owf english?
– an English programme?	Haben Sie ein Programm auf englisch?
	harben zee ain program owf english?
– an English brochure?	Haben Sie eine Broschüre auf englisch?
	harben zee ainer broashoorer owf english?

● At the cinema most films are dubbed (*synchronisiert*). In larger towns and cities as well as art cinemas subtitled versions are often screened, advertised as *Original mit Untertiteln*.

Do you have this week's/month's entertainment guide?
Haben Sie den Veranstaltungskalender von dieser Woche/diesem Monat?
harben zee den fairan-shtaltoongs-kalen-der fon deezer vokher/deezem moanart?

What's on tonight?
Was für Veranstaltungen gibt es heute abend?
vass fuer fairan-shtal-toongen gipt es hoyter arbent?

We want to go to...
Wir möchten in den/ins/in die...
veer moekhten in dayn/ins/in dee...

Which films are showing?
Welche Filme werden gespielt?
velkher filmer vairden geshpeelt?

What sort of film is that?
Was für ein Film ist das?
vass fuer ain film ist dass?

rated suitable for all the family
für jedes Alter
fuer yaydez alter

not suitable for children under 12/16 years
ab 12/16 Jahre(n)
ap tsvoelf/zekh tsayn yahre(n)

original version
Originalfassung
origginaal-fassoong

subtitled
untertitelt
oonter-teetelt

dubbed
synchronisiert
suen-khro-nee-zeert

What's on at...?
Was gibt es in...?
vass gipt es in...?

– the theatre?
Was gibt es im Theater?
vass gipt es im tayarter?

– the concert hall?	Was gibt es in der Konzerthalle/im Konzertsaal?
	vass gipt es in dayr kontsert-haller/im kontsert-zarl?
– the opera?	Was gibt es in der Oper?
	vass gipt es in dayr oaper?
Where can I find a good nightclub around here?	Wo gibt es einen guten Nachtklub?
	vo gipt es ainen gooten nakht-kloop?
Is it members only?	Muss man Mitglied sein?
	mooss man mittgleet zain?
Is it evening wear only?	Ist Abendkleidung Zwang?
	ist arbent-klai-doong tsvang?
Should I/we dress up?	Ist Abendkleidung erwünscht?
	ist arbent-klai-doong errvuensht?
What time does the show start?	Wann beginnt die Show?
	vann begint dee shoa?
When's the next football match?	Wann ist das nächste Fussballspiel?
	van ist dass nekster foos-barl-shpeel?
Who's playing?	Wer spielt gegen wen?
	vayr shpeelt gaygen vayn?

11.3 Booking tickets

Could you book some tickets for us?	Können Sie für uns reservieren?
	koennen zee fuer oons rezerveeren?
We'd like to book... seats/a table...	Wir möchten...Plätze/einen Tisch... reservieren
	veer moekhten...pletzer/ainen tish... rezerveeren
– in the stalls.	Wir möchten...Plätze/einen Tisch im Parkett reservieren.
	veer moekhten...pletzer/ainen tish im parkett rezerveeren

– on the balcony.	Wir möchten...Balkonplätze/einen Tisch auf dem Balkon reservieren.
	veer moekhten...balkoanpletzer/ainen tish owf daym balkoan rezerveeren
– box seats.	Wir möchten...Logenplätze reservieren.
	veer moekhten...loagen-pletzer rezerveeren
– a table at the front.	Bitte Plätze vorn.
	bitter pletser forn
– in the middle.	Bitte Plätze in der Mitte.
	bitter pletser in der mitter
– at the back.	Bitte Plätze hinten.
	bitter pletser hinten

Für welche Vorstellung möchten Sie reservieren?	Which performance do you want to book for?
Welche Plätze bitte?	Where would you like to sit?
Die Vorstellung ist ausverkauft.	Everything's sold out.
Es gibt nur noch Stehplätze.	It's standing room only.
Es gibt nur noch Balkonplätze... gibt es noch eine Sondervorstellung.	We've only got balcony seats. left...there is another special performance.
Es gibt nur noch Plätze im Parkett.	We've only got stalls seats left.
Es gibt nur noch Plätze in den vorderen Reihen.	We've only got seats left in the front rows.
Es gibt nur noch Plätze in den hinteren Reihen.	We've only got seats left in the back rows.
Wieviel Plätze wünschen Sie?	How many seats would you like?
Sie müssen die Karten vor...Uhr abholen.	You'll have to pick up the tickets before...o'clock.
Ihre Eintrittskarten bitte	Tickets, please.
Sie sitzen auf den falschen Plätzen.	You're in the wrong seats.

Could I book...seats for the... o'clock performance?

Kann ich...Plätze für die Vorstellung von... Uhr reservieren lassen?

kan ikh...pletser fuer dee for shtel loong fon...oohr rezerveeren lassen?

Are there any seats left for tonight?

Gibt es noch Karten für heute abend?

gipt es nokh karten fuer hoyter arbent?

How much is a ticket?

Wieviel kostet eine Karte?

veefeel kostet ainer karter?

When can I pick the tickets up?

Wann kann ich die Karten abholen?

van kan ikh dee karten aphoalen?

I've got a reservation.

Ich habe reserviert.

ikh harber rezerveert

My name's...

Mein Name ist...

main narmer ist...

12. Sports

12.1 Sporting questions

Where can we...around here?	Wo können wir hier...?
	vo koennen veer heer...?
Is there a...around here?	Gibt es hier in der Nähe ein(en)/eine...?
	gipt es heer in dayr nayher ain(en)/ainer...?
Can I hire a...here?	Kann ich hier ein(en)/eine...mieten/leihen?
	kan ikh heer ain(en)/ainer...meeten/laihen?
Can I take...lessons?	Kann ich...Stunden nehmen?
	kan ikh...shtoonden naymen?
How much is that per hour/per day/a turn?	Wieviel kostet das pro Stunde/Tag/Mal?
	veefeel kostet dass pro shtoonder/tark/marl?
Do I need a permit for that?	Braucht man dafür einen Schein/eine Genehmigung?
	browkht man darfuer ainen shain/ainer genay-mi-goong?
Where can I get the permit?	Wo kann ich die Genehmigung bekommen?
	vo kan ikh dee genay-mi-goong bekommen?

Is it a long way to the sea still?	Ist es noch weit bis ans Meer?
	ist es nokh vait biss ans meer?
Is there a...around here?	Gibt es hier in der Nähe ein... ?
	gipt es heer in dayr nayher ain... ?
– a public swimming pool	Gibt es hier in der Nähe ein Freibad (openair pool)/ Hallenbad (indoor pool)/ eine Badeanstalt? (public pool)
	gipt es heer in dayr nayher ain fraibart/ ainer hallen-bart/ainer barder-an-shalt?
– a sandy beach?	Gibt es hier in der Nähe einen Sandstrand?
	gipt ez heer in dayr nayher ainen sant-shtrant?
– a nudist beach?	Gibt es hier in der Nähe einen Nacktbadestrand?
	gipt ez heer in dayr nayher ainen nakt barder-shtrant?
– mooring?	Gibt es hier in der Nähe einen Anlegeplatz?
	gipt ez heer in dayr nayher ainen anlayger-plats?
Are there any rocks here?	Sind hier Felsen?
	zint heer felzen?
When's high/low tide?	Wann ist Flut/Ebbe?
	van ist floot/ebber?
What's the water temperature?	Welche Temperatur hat das Wasser?
	velkher temperatoor hat dass vasser?
Is it (very) deep here?	Ist es hier (sehr) tief?
	ist ez heer (zayr) teef?
Can you stand here?	Kann man hier stehen?
	kan man heer shtayen?

Achtung! Gefahr!	Angeln verboten	Nur mit
Danger	No fishing	Genehmigung
Angeln erlaubt	Baden verboten	Permits only
Fishing water	No swimming	Surfen verboten
		No surfing

Is it safe to swim here?

Kann man/(können Kinder) hier
ungefährdet schwimmen?
*kan man/(koennen kinder) heer
ungefayrdet shvimmen?*

Are there any currents?

Gibt es Strömungen?
gipt ez shtroe-moongen?

Are there any rapids/
waterfalls in this river?

Hat dieser Fluss Stromschnellen/
Wasserfälle?
*hat deezer flooss shtrom-shnellen/
vasser-feller?*

What does that flag/
buoy mean?

Was bedeutet die Flagge/Boje dort?
vass bedoytet dee flagger/boayer dort?

Is there a lifeguard on
duty here?

Gibt es hier einen Bademeister, der
aufpasst?
*gipt es heer ainen bardermaister, der
owfpasst?*

Are dogs allowed here?

Sind hier Hunde erlaubt?
zint heer hoonder erlowpt?

Is camping on the
beach allowed?

Darf man hier am Strand campen?
darf man heer am shtrant kampen?

Are we allowed to build
a fire here?

Darf man hier Feuer machen?
darf man heer foyer makhen?

Can I take ski lessons here?	Kann ich hier Skistunden nehmen?
	kan ikh heer shee-shtoonden naymen?
for beginners/advanced	für Anfänger/(etwas) Fortgeschrittene
	fuer anfenger/(etvass) fortgeshrittenner
How large are the groups?	Wie gross sind die Gruppen?
	vee groass zint dee grooppen?
What language are the classes in?	In welcher Sprache werden die Stunden gegeben?
	in velkher shprakher verden dee shtoonden gegayben?
I'd like a lift pass, please.	Ich möchte einen Ski(lift)pass.
	ikh moekhter ainen shee(lift)pass
Must I give you a passport photo?	Muss ich ein Passbild abgeben?
	mooss ikh ain passbilt apgayben?
Where are the beginners' slopes?	Wo sind die Skipisten für Anfänger? ((jokey): Wo ist der Idiotenhügel?)
	vo zint dee shee pisten fuer anfenger?
	vo ist dayr eedeeoa ten huegel?
Are there any runs for cross-country skiing?	Gibt es hier in der Nähe Loipen?
	gipt ez heer in dayr nayher loypen?
Have the cross-country runs been marked?	Sind die Loipen beschildert?
	zint dee loypen beshildert?
Are the...in operation?	Sind die...geöffnet?
	zint dee...geoeffnet?
– the ski lifts	Sind die Skilifte geöffnet?
	zint dee sheelifter geoeffnet?
– the chair lifts	Sind die Sessellifte geöffnet?
	zint dee zessel-lifter geoeffnet?
Are the slopes usable?	Sind die Pisten offen?
	zint dee pisten offen?
Are the cross-country runs usable?	Sind die Loipen offen?
	zint dee loypen offen?

13. Sickness

13.1 Call (fetch) the doctor

Could you call/fetch a doctor
  quickly, please?

Rufen/holen Sie bitte schnell einen Arzt?
  *roofen/hoalen zee bitter shnell ainen
    artst?*

When does the doctor
  have surgery?

Wann hat der Arzt Sprechstunde?
  van hat dayr artst shprekh shtoonder?

When can the doctor come?

Wann kann der Arzt kommen?
  van kan dayr artst kommen?

I'd like to make an
  appointment to see
  the doctor.

Können Sie für mich einen Termin beim
  Arzt machen?
  *koennen zee fuer mikh ainen tairmeen
    baim artst makhen?*

I've got an appointment to
  see the doctor at…

Ich habe um…Uhr einen Termin
  beim Arzt.
  *ikh harber oom…ooer ainen tairmeen
    baim artst*

Which doctor/chemist has
  night/weekend duty?

Welcher Arzt/welche Apotheke hat
  Nachtdienst/Notdienst?
  *velkher artst/velkher apotayker hat nakht
    deenst/noat-deenst?*

13.2 Patient's ailments

I don't feel well.

Ich fühle mich unwohl.
  ikh fueler mikh oonvoal

I'm dizzy.

Mir ist schwindlig.
  meer ist shvindlikh

- ill.

Ich bin krank.
  ikh bin krank

- sick.

Mir ist schlecht/übel.
  meer ist shlekht/uebel

I've got a cold.

Ich bin erkältet.
  ikh bin erkelltet

It hurts here.

Ich habe hier Schmerzen.
  ikh harber heer shmertsen

I've been throwing up.	Ich habe mich übergeben.
	ikh harber mikh uebergayben
I've got...	Ich habe...Beschwerden.
	ikh harber...beshverden
I'm running a temperature.	Ich habe...(Grad) Fieber.
	ikh harber...(grart) feeber
I've been stung by a wasp.	Ich bin von einer Wespe gestochen worden.
	ikh bin fon ainer vesper geshtokhen vorden
I've been stung by an insect.	Ein Insekt hat mich gestochen oder gebissen.
	ain inzekt hat mikh geshtokhen oader gebissen
I've been bitten by a dog.	Mich hat ein Hund gebissen.
	mikh hat ain hoont gebissen
I've been stung by a jellyfish.	Mich hat eine Qualle gestochen.
	mikh hat ainer kvaller geshtokhen
I've been bitten by a snake.	Mich hat eine Schlange gebissen.
	mikh hat ainer shlanger gebissen
I've been bitten by an animal.	Mich hat ein Tier gebissen.
	mikh hat ain teer gebissen
I've cut myself.	Ich habe mich geschnitten.
	ikh harber mikh geshnitten
I've burned myself.	Ich habe mich verbrannt.
	ikh harber mikh fayrbrant
I've grazed myself.	Ich habe eine Hautabschürfung.
	ikh harber ainer howt ap shuer foong
I've had a fall.	Ich bin gestürzt.
	ikh bin geshtuertst
I've sprained my ankle.	Ich habe mir den Knöchel verstaucht.
	ikh harber meer den knoekhel fairshtowkht
I've come for the morning-after pill.	Ich möchte die 'Pille danach'.
	ikh moekhter dee 'piller darnakh'

Was für Beschwerden haben Sie? (Wo fehlt's denn?)	What seems to be the problem?
Wie lange haben Sie diese Beschwerden schon?	How long have you had these symptoms?
Haben Sie diese Beschwerden schonfrüher gehabt?	Have you had this trouble before?
Wie hoch ist das Fieber?	How high is your temperature?
Machen Sie sich bitte frei.	Get undressed, please.
Machen Sie bitte den Oberkörper frei.	Strip to the waist, please.
Sie können sich dort ausziehen/ freimachen.	You can undress there.
Bitte machen Sie den linken/ rechten Arm frei.	Roll up your left/right sleeve, please.
Legen Sie sich hierauf.	Lie down here, please.
Tut das weh?/Haben Sie hier Schmerzen?	Does this hurt?
Tief ein- und ausatmen.	Breathe deeply.
Öffnen Sie den Mund.	Open your mouth.

Patient's medical history

I'm a diabetic.	Ich bin zuckerkrank/Diabetiker.
	ikh bin tsooker-krank/deea-bayt-ikker
I have a heart condition.	Ich bin herzkrank/Ich habe ein Herzleiden.
	ikh bin hairtskrank/ikh harber ain hertslaiden
I have asthma.	Ich habe Asthma/Ich bin Asthmatiker.
	ikh harber astmar/ikh bin astmartikker
I'm allergic to...	Ich bin allergisch gegen...
	ikh bin allairgish gaygen...

Sind Sie gegen irgendetwas allergisch?	Do you have any allergies?
Nehmen Sie Medikamente (ein)?	Are you on any medication?
Haben Sie eine Diät?	Are you on a diet?
Sind Sie schwanger?	Are you pregnant?
Sind Sie gegen Wundstarrkrampf geimpft?	Have you had a tetanus injection?

Es ist nichts Ernstes.	It's nothing serious.
Sie haben sich den/die/das... gebrochen.	Your...is broken.
Sie haben sich den/die/das... verstaucht.	You've sprained...
Sie haben einen Riss...	You've got (a) torn...
Sie haben eine Entzündung.	You've got an inflammation.
Sie haben Blinddarmentzündung.	You've got appendicitis.
Sie haben Bronchitis.	You've got bronchitis.
Sie haben eine Geschlechtskrankheit.	You've got a venereal disease.
Sie haben Grippe.	You've got the flu.
Sie haben einen Herzanfall gehabt.	You've had a heart attack.
Sie haben eine Infektion (Virus, bakterielle).	You've got an infection (viral, bacterial).
Sie haben Lungenentzündung.	You've got pneumonia.
Sie haben ein Magengeschwür.	You've got an ulcer.
Sie haben eine Muskelzerrung.	You've pulled a muscle.

Sie haben eine vaginale Entzündung.	You've got a vaginal infection.
Sie haben eine Lebensmittelvergiftung/ Nahrungs-mittelvergiftung.	You've got food poisoning.
Sie haben einen Sonnenstich.	You've got sunstroke.
Sie sind allergisch gegen...	You're allergic to...
Sie sind schwanger.	You're pregnant.
Ich möchte eine Blut/Harn/ Stuhluntersuchung machen lassen.	I'd like to have your blood/urine/ stools tested.
Es muss genäht werden.	It needs stitching.
Ich schicke Sie zu einem Facharzt/ins Krankenhaus/ Hospital.	I'm referring you to a specialist/ sending you to hospital.
Es müssen Röntgenaufnahmen gemacht werden.	You'll need to have some x-rays taken.
Setzen Sie sich bitte (wieder) ins Wartezimmer.	Could you wait in the waiting room, please?
Sie müssen operiert werden.	You'll need an operation.

'm...months pregnant.	Ich bin...Monate schwanger.
	ikh bin...moanarter shvan
'm on a diet.	Ich habe eine Diät.
	ikh harber ainer deeyayt
'm on medication/the pill.	Ich nehme Medikamente/die Pille.
	ikh naymer medee ker menter/dee piller
've had a heart attack once before.	Ich habe schon mal einen Herzanfall gehabt.
	ikh harber shoan mall ainen hertsanfall gehapt
've had a(n)...operation.	Ich bin am/an der...operiert.
	ikh bin am/an dayr...opereert

I've been ill recently.	Ich bin gerade krank gewesen.
	ikh bin gerarder krank gevayzen
I've got an ulcer.	Ich habe ein Magengeschwür.
	ikh harber ain margen-geshvuer
I've got my period.	Ich habe meine Periode.
	ikh harber mainer peree-oader

The diagnosis

Is it contagious?	Ist es ansteckend?
	ist ez anshtekkent?
How long do I have to stay...?	Wie lange muss ich...bleiben?
	vee langer mooss ikh...blaiben?
– in bed?	Wie lange muss ich im Bett bleiben?
	vee langer mooss ikh im bett blaiben?
– in hospital?	Wie lange muss ich im Krankenhaus bleiben?
	vee langer mooss ikh im kranken-howz blaiben?
Do I have to go on a special diet?	Muss ich eine Diät einhalten?
	mooss ikh ainer deeyayt ainhalten?
Am I allowed to travel?	Darf ich reisen?
	darf ikh raizen?
Can I make a new appointment?	Kann ich einen neuen Termin machen?
	kan ikh ainen noyen termeen makhen?
When do I have to come back?	Wann soll ich wiederkommen?
	van zoll ikh veeder-kommen?
I'll come back tomorrow.	Ich komme morgen wieder.
	ikh kommer morgen veeder

Kommen Sie morgen/in... Tagen wieder	Come back tomorrow/in... days' time

Ich verschreibe Ihnen ein Antibiotikum/einen Saft/ ein Beruhigungsmittel/ Schmerzmittel.	I'm prescribing antibiotics/a mixture/a tranquillizer/painkillers.
Sie dürfen sich nicht anstrengen/Sie müssen sich schonen.	Have lots of rest.
Sie dürfen nicht nach draussen.	Stay indoors.
Sie müssen im Bett bleiben.	Stay in bed.

alle...Stunden	Kapseln	Spritzen
every...hours	capsules	injections
die Kur beenden	Löffel (Ess-/Tee-)	Tabletten
finish the course	spoonfuls	tablets
dieses Medikament beeinträchtigt die Fahrtüchtigkeit	(tablespoons/ teaspoons)	Tropfen
this medication impairs your driving	...mal täglich	drops
einnehmen	...times a day	vor jeder Mahlzeit
take	nicht zerkauen	before meals
einreiben	do not chew	während...Tagen
rub on	nur für äusserliche Anwendung	for...days
in Wasser (auf)lösen	for external use only	Zäpfchen
dissolve in water	Salbe	suppository
	ointment	

How do I take this medicine?	Wie soll ich diese Medikamente einnehmen?
	vee zoll ikh deezer medee-kar-menter ain naymen?

151

How many capsules/drops/ injections/spoonfuls/ tablets each time?	Wieviel Kapseln/Tropfen/Spritzen/Löffel/ Tabletten/Zäpfchen pro Mal?
	veefeel kapseln/tropfen/shpritsen/ loeffel/ tabletten/tsepfkhen pro marl?
How many times a day?	Wie oft täglich?
	vee oft tayglikh?
I've forgotten my medication. At home I take…	Ich habe meine Medikamente vergessen.
	Zu hause nehme ich…ikh harber mainer medee-kar-menter fairgessen. tsoo howzer naymer ikh…
Could you make out a prescription for me?	Können Sie mir ein Rezept ausstellen?
	koennen zee meer ain retsept ows shtellen?

13.5 At the dentist's

Do you know a good dentist?	Können Sie mir einen guten Zahnarzt/ Dentisten empfehlen?
	koennen zee meer ainen gooten tsarn- artst/denteesten empfaylen?
Could you make a dentist's appointment for me? It's urgent.	Können Sie mir einen Termin beim Zahnarzt besorgen? Es eilt.
	koennen zee meer ainen termeen baim tsarn-artst bezorgen? ez ailt
Can I come in today, please?	Könnte ich bitte heute noch kommen?
	koennter ikh bitter hoyter nokh kommen?
I have (terrible) toothache.	Ich habe (schreckliche) Zahnschmerzen.
	ikh harber (shrek likher) tsarn-shmertsen
Could you prescribe/give me a painkiller?	Können Sie mir ein Schmerzmittel verschreiben/geben?
	koennen zee meer ain shmairts mittel fair-shraiben/gayben?
A piece of my tooth has broken off.	Mir ist ein Stück vom Zahn/Backenzahn abgebrochen.
	meer ist ain shtuek fom tsarn/ bakkentsarn apgebrokhen

My filling's come out.	Ich habe eine Füllung verloren.
	ikh harber ainer fuellung fairloren
I've got a broken crown.	Mir ist eine Krone abgebrochen.
	meer ist ainer kroner apgebrokhen
I'd like/I don't want a local anaesthetic.	Ich möchte (nicht) örtlich betäubt werden.
	ikh moekhter (nikht) oertlikh betoypt verden
Can you do a makeshift repair job?	Können Sie mir jetzt provisorisch helfen?
	koennen zee meer yetst provee-zorish helfen?
I don't want this tooth pulled.	Ich will nicht, dass dieser Zahn gezogen wird.
	ikh vill nikht, dass deezer tsarn getsoagen virt
My dentures are broken. Can you fix them?	Mein Gebiss ist zerbrochen. Können Sie es reparieren?
	main gebiss ist tsayrbrokhen. koennen zee es repareeren?

☞

Welcher Zahn/(Backenzahn) tut weh?	Which tooth hurts?
Sie haben ein(en) Abszess.	You've got an abscess.
Ich muss eine Nervenbehandlung machen/durchführen.	I'll have to do a root canal.
Ich betäube Sie örtlich.	I'm giving you a local anaesthetic.
Ich muss diesen...füllen/ziehen/ abschleifen.	I'll have to fill/pull/file this tooth.
Ich muss bohren.	I'll have to drill.
Mund auf, bitte.	Open wide, please.
Mund zu, bitte.	Close your mouth, please.
Spülen, bitte.	Rinse, please.
Tut es noch weh?	Does it hurt still?

14. In trouble

Help!	Hilfe!
	hillfer!
Fire!	Feuer!
	foyer!
Police!	Polizei!
	poleetsai!
Quick!	Schnell!
	shnell!
Danger!	Gefahr!
	gefahr!
Watch out!	Achtung!
	akhtoong!
Stop!	Halt!
	halt!
Be careful!	Vorsicht!
	forzikht!
Don't!	Nicht tun!
	nikht toon!
Let go!	Loslassen!
	loaslassen!
Stop that thief!	Haltet den Dieb!
	haltet den deep!
Could you help me, please?	Würden Sie mir bitte helfen?
	vuerden zee meer bitter helfen?
Where's the police station/ emergency exit/fire escape?	Wo ist die Polizeiwache/der Notausgang/ die Feuertreppe?
	vo ist dee polee-tsai-vakher/der noat-ows gang/dee foyer-trepper?
Where's the nearest fire extinguisher?	Wo ist ein Feuerlöscher?
	vo ist ain foyer-loesher?
Call the fire brigade!	Rufen Sie die Feuerwehr!
	roofen zee dee foyer-vair!

Call the police!	Rufen Sie die Polizei (an)!
	roofen zee dee poleetsai (an)
Call an ambulance!	Rufen Sie einen Krankenwagen/ Rettungswagen!
	roofen zee ainen krunken-vargen/ rettoongs vargen
Where's the nearest phone?	Wo gibt's ein Telefon?
	vo gipt's ain telefoan?
Could I use your phone?	Darf ich Ihr Telefon benutzen?
	darf ikh eer telefoan benootsen?
What's the emergency number?	Wie lautet die Alarmnummer?
	vee lowtet dee alarm-noomer?
What's the number for the police?	Wie ist die Telefonnummer der Polizei?
	vee ist dee telefoan-noomer dayr poleetsai?

14.2 Loss

I've lost my purse/wallet/ mobile phone/passport	Ich habe mein Portemonnaie/meine Brieftasche/Handy/Reisepass verloren
	ikh harber main portmonnay/mainer breeftasher fairloren
I lost my...yesterday.	Ich habe gestern mein(en)/meine... vergessen.
	ikh harber gestern main(en)/mainer... fairgessen
I left my...here.	Ich habe hier mein(en)/meine... liegengelassen/stehengelassen.
	ikh harber heer main(en)/mainer...leegen gelassen/shtayen-gelassen
Did you find my...?	Haben Sie mein(en)/meine...gefunden?
	harben zee main(en)/mainer... gefoonden?
It was right here.	Er/sie/es stand/lag hier.
	er/zee/es shtant/lark heer

It's quite valuable. Es ist sehr wertvoll.
ez ist zayr vayrtfoll

Where's the lost Wo ist das Fundbüro?
property office? *vo ist dass funt-buero?*

14.3 Accidents

There's been an accident. Es ist ein Unfall passiert.
ez ist ain unfarl passeert

Someone's fallen into Jemand ist ins Wasser gefallen.
the water. *yaymant ist ins vasser gefallen*

There's a fire. Es brennt.
ez brennt

Is anyone hurt? Ist jemand verletzt?
ist yaymant fairletst?

Some people have been/ Es gibt (keine) Verletzte(n).
no one's been injured. *ez gipt (kainer) fairletste(n)*

There's someone in the Es ist noch jemand im Auto/Zug.
car/train still. *ez ist nokh yaymant im owto/tsook*

It's not too bad. Don't worry. Es ist nicht so schlimm. Machen Sie sich
keine Sorgen.
ez ist nikht zo shlimm. makhen zee zikh
kainer zorgen

Leave everything the way Lassen Sie bitte alles, so wie es ist.
it is, please. *lassen zee bitter alles, zo vee ez ist*

I want to talk to the police first. Ich will erst mit der Polizei sprechen.
ikh vill airst mit dayr poleetsai shprekhen

I want to take a photo first. Ich will erst ein Foto machen.
ikh vill airst ain foto makhen

Here's my name and address. Hier sind mein Name und meine
Adresse.
*heer zint main narmer unt mainer
adresser*

Could I have your name and address?	Geben Sie mir bitte Ihren Namen und Ihre Adresse?
	gayben zee meer bitter eeren narmen unt eerer adresser
Could I see some identification/ your insurance papers?	Dürfte ich Ihren Ausweis/Ihre Versicherungspapiere sehen?
	duerfter ikh eeren owsvais/eerer fairzikheroongs-papeerer zayhen?
Will you act as a witness?	Wollen Sie Zeuge sein?
	vollen zee tsoyger zain?
I need the details for the insurance.	Ich brauche die Angaben für die Versicherung.
	ikh browkher dee angarben fuer dee fairzikhe-roong
Are you insured?	Sind Sie versichert?
	zint zee fairzikhert?
Third party or comprehensive?	Haftpflicht oder Vollkasko-Versicherung?
	haftpflikht oader follkassko-fairzikhe-roong?
Could you sign here, please?	Unterschreiben Sie hier bitte.
	oonter shraiben zee heer bitter

14.4 Theft

I've been robbed.	Ich bin bestohlen worden.
	ikh bin beshtoalen vorden
My...has been stolen.	Mein(e) ... ist gestohlen worden.
	main(er) ... ist geshtoalen vorden
My car's been broken into.	Mein Auto ist aufgebrochen worden.
	main owto ist owfgebrokhen vorden
My room has been broken into.	In mein Zimmer wurde eingebrochen.
	in main tsimmair woorder aingebrokhen.

14.5 Missing person

I've lost my child/grandmother.
Mein Kind/meine Oma ist verschwunden.
main kint/mainer oamar ist fairshvoonden

Could you help me find him/her?
Würden Sie mir bitte suchen helfen?
vuerden zee meer bitter zookhen helfen?

Have you seen a small child?
Haben Sie ein kleines Kind gesehen?
harben zee ain klaines kint gezayhen?

He's/she's...years old.
Er/sie ist...Jahre.
er/zee ist...yahrer

He's/she's got short/long/ blond/red/brown/black/ grey/curly/ straight/ frizzy hair.
Er/sie hat kurzes/langes/blondes/rotes/ braunes/schwarzes/graues/lockiges/ glattes/gekräu seltes Haar.
er/zee hat koortses/langes/blondes/ roates/ brownes/shvartses/growes/ lokigges/glattes/gekroyzeltes har.

with a ponytail
mit Pferdeschwanz
mit pferder-shvants

with plaits
mit Zöpfen
mit tsoepfen

in a bun
mit einem Knoten/Dutt
mit ainem knooten/doott

He's/she's got blue/ brown/green eyes.
Die Augen sind blau/braun/grün.
dee owgen zint blow/brown/gruen

He's wearing swimming trunks/mountaineering boots.
Er trägt eine Badehose/Wanderschuhe.
er traykht ainer barder-hoazer/ vander-shooer

with/without glasses
mit/ohne Brille
mit/oaner briller

tall/short
gross/klein
groass/klain

This is a photo of him/her.
Hier ist ein Bild von ihm/ihr.
heer ist ain bilt fon eem/eer

He/she must be lost.
Er/sie hat sich sicher verlaufen.
er/zee hat zikh zikher fairlowfen

14.6 The police

An arrest

Ihre Fahrzeugpapiere bitte.	Your registration papers, please.
Sie sind zu schnell gefahren.	You were speeding.
Sie parken falsch.	You're not allowed to park here.
Sie haben kein Geld in die Parkuhr gesteckt.	You haven't put money in the meter.
Ihr Licht brennt nicht.	Your lights aren't working.
Sie müssen einen Alkoholtest abgeben.	You must give a breathalyser test.
Sie bekommen eine gebühren-pflichtige Verwarnung/ einen Strafzettel von...	You are to receive a fine of/a parking ticket for...
Zahlen Sie sofort?	Do you want to pay on the spot?
Sie müssen sofort bezahlen.	You'll have to pay on the spot.

I don't speak German.	Ich spreche kein Deutsch.
	ikh shprekher kain doytsh
I didn't see the sign.	Ich habe das Schild nicht gesehen.
	ikh harber das shilt nikht gezayhen
I don't understand what it says.	Ich verstehe nicht, was da steht.
	ikh fairshtayher nikht, vass dar shtayt
I was only doing...kilometres an hour.	Ich bin nur...Kilometer pro Stunde gefahren.
	ikh bin noor...keelomayter pro shtoonder gefahren
I'll have my car checked.	Ich werde mein Auto nachsehen lassen.
	ikh verder main owto nakh zayhen lassen
I was blinded by oncoming lights.	Der Gegenverkehr hat mich geblendet.
	dayr gaygen fairkair hat mikh geblendet

At the police station

Wo ist es passiert?	Where did it happen?
Was haben Sie verloren?	What's missing?
Was ist gestohlen (worden)?	What's been taken?
Ihren Ausweis bitte.	Could I see some identification?
Wann ist es passiert?	What time did it happen?
Wer war daran beteiligt?	Who was involved?
Gibt es Zeugen?	Are there any witnesses?
Bitte füllen Sie das aus.	Fill this out, please.
Hier bitte unterschreiben.	Sign here, please.
Möchten Sie einen Dolmetscher?	Do you want an interpreter?

want to report a collision/
something missing/missing
person.

Ich möchte einen Zusammenstoss/
einen Verlust (things missing)/
Ich möchte eine Vermisstenanzeige
(persons missing) machen.

*ikh moekhter ainen tsoo-zammen
shtoas/ainen fairloost/ikh moekhter
ainer fayrmissten antsaiger makhen*

– a robbery/mugging/assault ein Raub/Überfall/tätlicher Angriff

ain rowb/uebairful/taytlishair ungrif

– a rape eine Vergewaltigung anzeigen

ainer fair-gevalti-goong an-tsaigen

Could you make out a
report, please?

Würden Sie bitte ein Protokoll
aufnehmen?

*vuerden zee bitter ain proatoakoll
owfnaymen?*

Could I have a copy for
the insurance?

Geben Sie mir bitte eine Abschrift für die
Versicherung

*gayben zee meer bitter ainer apshrift fuer
dee fair-zeekhe-roong*

've lost everything. Ich habe alles verloren.

ikh harber alles fairloren

All my money is gone, I don't know what to do.	Mein Geld ist alle, ich bin ratlos. *main gelt ist aller, ikh bin rartloas*
Could you please lend me some?	Könnten Sie mir bitte etwas leihen? *koennten zee meer bitter etvass laihen?*
I'd like an interpreter.	Ich möchte einen Dolmetscher. *ikh moekhter ainen dolmetsher*
I'm innocent.	Ich bin unschuldig. *ikh bin oonshuldikh*
I don't know anything about it.	Ich weiss von nichts. *ikh vaiss fon nikhts*
I want to speak to someone from the British consulate.	Ich möchte jemanden vom britischen Konsulat sprechen. *ikh moekhter yaymanden fom breetishen konsoolart shprekhen*
I need to see someone from the British embassy.	Ich möchte jemanden von der britischen Botschaft sprechen. *ikh moekhter yaymunden fon dayr breetishen boatshaft shprekhen*
I want a lawyer who speaks...	Ich will einen Rechtsanwalt, der...spricht. *ikh vill ainen rekhts anvalt, dayr...shprikht*

15. Word list

Word list English–German

● This word list supplements the previous chapters. Nouns are always accompanied by the German definite article in order to indicate whether it is a masculine (der), feminine (die), or a neuter (das) word. In a number of cases, words not contained in this list can be found elsewhere in this book, namely in the lists of the parts of the car and the bicycle (both **Section 5**) and the tent **(Section 7)**. Many food terms can be found in the German-English Menu Reader in **Section 4.7**.

A

about	ungefähr	oongefayr
above	über	ueber
abroad	das Ausland	dass owslant
accident	der Unfall	dayr oonfarl
adder	die Natter	dee natter
addition	die Addition	dee adittseeyoan
address	die Adresse	dee adresser
admission	der Eintritt	dayr aintritt
admission price	der Eintrittspreis	dayr aintritts-praiss
advice	der Rat	dayr rart
after	nach	nakh
afternoon	mittags	mittargs
aftershave	die After-shave-Lotion	dee after-shave loatseeyown
again	erneut	ayrnoyt
against	gegen	gaygen
age	das Alter	dass alter
air conditioning	die Klimaanlage	dee kleemaranlarger
air mattress	die Luftmatratze	dee looft-mattratser
air sickness bag	die Spucktüte	dee shpook-tueter
aircraft	das Flugzeug	dass flooktsoyk
airport	der Flughafen	dayr flookharfen
alarm	der Alarm	dayr alarm
alarm clock	der Wecker	dayr vekker

alcohol	der Alkohol	*dayr alkohol*
allergic	allergisch	*allayrgish*
alone	allein	*allain*
always	immer	*immer*
ambulance	der Rettungswagen	*dayr rettoongs-vargen*
amount	der Betrag	*dayr betrarg*
amusement park	der Vergnügungs park	*dayr fayr-gnue-goongs park*
anchovy	die Anschovis	*dee antshoveez*
and	und	*oont*
angry	böse	*boezer*
animal	das Tier	*dass teer*
ankle	der Knöchel	*dayr knoekhel*
answer	die Antwort	*dee antvort*
ant	die Ameise	*dee armaizer*
antibiotics	das Antibiotikum	*dass antee-beeotee-kum*
antifreeze	das Frostschutzmittel	*dass frost-shoots-mittel*
antique	alt/(books) antiquarisch	*alt/anteekvarish*
antiques	die Antiquität	*dee antee-kveetayt*
antiseptic cream	antiseptische Creme	*untiseptishe krem*
anus	der After	*dayr after*
apartment	das Appartement	*dass appartamong*
aperitif	der Aperitif	*dayr appereeteef*
apologies	die Entschuldigung	*dee ent-shooldigoong*
apple	der Apfel	*dayr apfel*
apple juice	der Apfelsaft	*dayr apfelzaft*
apple pie	der Apfelkuchen	*dayr apfel-kookhen*
apple sauce	das Apfelmus	*dass apfel-moos*
appointment	der Termin	*dayr termeen*
apricot	die Aprikose	*dee apree koazer*
	die Marille (Aus.)	*dee mariller*
April	der April	*dayr aprill*
Archbishop	der Erzbischof	*dayr airts-bishoaf*
architecture	die Architektur	*dee arkhee tektoor*
area	die Umgebung	*dee oom gay boong*
arena	die Manege	*dee manerjer*
arm	der Arm	*dayr arm*
arrange	(sich) verabreden	*(sikh) fayr-aprayden*

arrive	ankommen	ankommen
arrow	der Pfeil	dayr pfail
art	die Kunst	dee koonst
artery	die Schlagader	dee shlarkarder
artichokes	die Artischocke	dee artee shokker
article	der Artikel	dayr arteekel
artificial respiration	die künstliche Beatmung	dee kuenstlikher beart moong
ashtray	der Aschenbecher	dayr ashenbekher
ask	fragen	frargen
ask for	bitten um	bitten oom
asparagus	der Spargel	dayr shpargel
aspirin	das Aspirin	dass asspireen
assault	die Vergewaltigung	dee fayr-gevaltee-goong
at home	zu Hause	tsoo howzer
at the front	vorn	forn
at the latest	spätestens	shpaytestenz
aubergine	die Aubergine	dee owberjeener
August	der August	dayr owgoost
automatic	automatisch	owtow-mar-teesh
autumn	der Herbst	dayr hayrpst
avalanche	die Lawine	dee laveener
awake	wach	varkh
awning	das Vordach	dass fordakh

B

baby	das Baby	dass baybee
baby food	die Babynahrung	dee baybee-nahroong
babysitter	der Babysitter	dayr baybee-zitter
back (at the)	hinten	hinten
back	der Rücken	dayr ruekken
bacon	der Speck	dayr shpek
bad	schlecht/schlimm	shlekht/shlim
bag	die Tasche	dee tasher
bakery	der Bäckerei	dee bekerai

balcony	der Balkon	*dayr balkoan*
ball	der Ball	*dayr barl*
ballet	das Ballett	*dass balett*
ballpoint pen	der Kugelschreiber/	*dayr koogel-shraiber/*
	der Kuli	*dayr koolee*
banana	die Banane	*dee banarner*
bandage	der Verband	*dayr fayrbant*
bank (river)	das Ufer	*dass oofer*
bank	die Bank	*dee bank*
bank pass	die Scheckkarte	*dee shekkarter*
bar	die Bar	*dee bar*
barbecue	das Barbecue	*dass barbekyu*
basketball (to play)	das Baskettballspiel	*dass basket-barl-shpeel*
bath	das Bad	*dass bart*
bath attendant	der Bademeister	*dayr barder-maister*
bath foam	das Schaumbad	*dass showmbart*
bath towel	das Handtuch/(large)	*dass hanttookh/*
	das Badelaken	*dass barder-larken*
bathing cap	die Badekappe	*dee barder-kapper*
bathing cubicle	die Badekabine	*dee barder-kabeener*
bathing suit	der Badeanzug	*dayr barder-antsook*
bathroom	das Badezimmer	*dass barder-tsimmer*
battery	die Batterie	*dee batteree*
be in love with	verliebt sein in	*fayrleept zain in*
beach	der Strand	*dayr shtrant*
beans	die Bohnen	*dee boanen*
beautiful	schön/prächtig	*shoen/prekhtikh*
beauty parlour	der Kosmetiksalon	*dayr kozmaytik-zalong*
bed	das Bett	*dass bett*
bee	die Biene	*dee beener*
beef	das Rindfleisch	*dass rintflaish*
beer	das Bier	*dass beer*
beetroot	die rote Bete	*dee roater bayter*
begin	anfangen/beginnen	*anfangen/beginnen*
beginner	der Anfänger	*dayr anfenger*
behind	hinter (prep.)/	*hinter/*
	hinten (adj.)	*hinten*

Belgian	der Belgier/	dayr bellgiyer/
	die Belgierin	dee bellgiyerin
Belgium	Belgien	bellgiyen
belt	der Gürtel	dayr guertel
berth	der Liegeplatz	dayr leeger-plats
better	besser	besser
bicycle	das Fahrrad	dass far-rart
bicycle pump	die Luftpumpe	dee looft-poomper
	(fürs Fahrrad)	(fuers far rart)
bicycle repairman	der Fahrradhändler	dayr farrart-hendler
bikini	der Bikini	dayr bikeeni
bill	die Rechnung	dee rekhnoong
billiards (to play)	Billard spielen	billyard shpeelen
birthday	der Geburtstag	dayr geboorts tark
biscuit	der Biskuit/der Keks	dayr biskveet/dayr keks
bite (to)	beissen	baissen
bitter	bitter	bitter
black	schwarz	shvarts
bland	geschmacklos	geshmakkloass
blanket	die Decke	dee dekker
bleach	blondieren	blondeeren
blister	die Blase	dee blarzer
blond	blond	blont
blood	das Blut	dass bloot
blood pressure	der Blutdruck	dayr bloot-drook
blouse	die Bluse	dee bloozer
blow dry	föhnen	foenen
blue	blau	blow
board (on)	an Bord	an bort
boat	das Boot	dass boat
body	der Körper	dayr koerper
body milk	die Bodylotion	dee body-loa-tseeoan
boiled	gekocht	gekokht
bonbon	die Praline/das Bonbon	dee praleener/dass bonbon
bone	der Knochen	dayr knokhen
bonnet	die Motorhaube	dee moator-howber
book (to)	reservieren	rezayrveeren

book	das Buch	*dass bookh*
booked	reserviert	*rezayrveert*
booking office	die Vorverkaufsstelle	*dee for-fayrkowfs-shteller*
bookshop	die Buchhandlung	*dee bookh-hand-loong*
border	die Grenze	*dee grentser*
bored (to be)	sich langweilen	*zikh langvailen*
boring	langweilig	*langvailikh*
born	geboren	*geboren*
borrow	ausleihen	*owslaihen*
botanical gardens	der Botanische Garten	*dayr boatarnisher garten*
both	beides	*baidez*
bottle	die Flasche	*dee flasher*
box	der Karton	*dayr karton*
box	die Loge	*dee loajer*
boy	der Junge	*dayr yoonger*
bra	der BH	*dayr bayhar*
bracelet	das Armband	*dass armbant*
braised	gedünstet/gesotten	*geduenstet/gezotten*
brake	die Bremse	*dee bremzer*
brake fluid	die Bremsflüssigkeit	*dee bremz-fluessikh-kait*
brake oil	das Bremsöl	*dass bremzoel*
bread	das Brot	*dass broat*
break	(zer-)brechen	*(tsair-)brekhen*
breakfast	das Frühstück	*dass frueshtuek*
breast	die Brust	*dee broost*
bridge	die Brücke	*dee brueker*
briefs	der Schlüpfer	*dayr shluepfer*
bring	(mit-)bringen	*(mit-)bringen*
brochure	die Broschüre	*dee broashuerer*
broken	kaputt	*kapoott*
brother	der Bruder	*dayr brooder*
brown	braun	*brown*
brush	die Bürste	*dee buerster*
Brussels sprouts	der Rosenkohl	*dayr rozenkoal*
bucket	der Eimer	*dayr aimer*
bug	das Ungeziefer	*dass oon-getseefer*
building	das Gebäude	*dass geboyder*

buoy	die Boje	*dee boayer*
burglary	der Einbruch	*dayr ainbrookh*
burn	verbrennen	*fair brennen*
burnt	angebrannt	*angebrant*
bus	der (Auto-)Bus	*dayr (owtoa-)-booss*
bus station	der Busbahnhof	*dayr booss-barnhoaf*
bus stop	die Bushaltestelle	*dee booss-halter-shteller*
business class	Business Class	*bizniss klarss*
business trip	die Geschäftsreise	*dee geshefts raizer*
busy	lebhaft/geschäftig	*layphaft/gesheftikh*
butane camping gas	das Butangas	*dass bootarn-gass*
butcher	der Schlachter/	*dayr shlakhter/*
	der Metzger	*dayr mettsger*
butter	die Butter	*dee booter*
button	der Knopf	*dayr knopf*
buy	kaufen	*kowfen*
by airmail	per Luftpost	*payr looftpost*

C

cabbage	der Kohl	*dayr koal*
cabin	die Kabine	*dee kabeener*
cake	der Kuchen/	*dayr kukhen/*
	das (Stück) Gebäck/	*dass (shtuek) gebeck*
	die Torte	*dee torter*
cake shop	die Konditorei	*dee kondeetorai*
call	anrufen	*anroofen*
called (to be)	heissen	*haissen*
camera	die Kamera	*dee kammerar*
camp	campen	*kampen*
camp shop	der Campingladen	*dayr kamping-larden*
camp site	der Campingplatz	*dayr kamping-plats*
camper	das Wohnmobil	*dass voan moabeel*
campfire	das Lagerfeuer	*dass larger-foyer*
camping guide	der Campingführer	*dayr kamping-fuerer*
camping permit	die Camping-erlaubnis	*dee kamping ayrlowpniss*

cancel (to)	annullieren	annooleeren
candle	die Kerze	dee kayrtser
canoe (to)	Kanu fahren	kanoo faren
canoe	das Kanu	dass kanoo
car	das Auto	dass owtoa
car deck	das Autodeck	dass owtoa-deck
car documents	die Fahrzeugpapiere	dee far-tsoyk-papeerer
car park	die Parkgarage	dee parkgararjer
(multi-storey)		
car seat	der Kindersitz	dayr kinderzits
car trouble	die Panne	dee panner
carafe	die Karaffe	dee karaffer
caravan	der Wohnwagen	dayr voan-vargen
cardigan	die Jacke	dee yakker
careful	vorsichtig	forzikhtikh
carrot	die Karotte	dee karotter
carton of cigarettes	die Stange Zigaretten	dee shtanger tsigaretten
cascade	der Wasserfall	dayr vasserfall
cash desk	die Kasse	dee kasser
casino	das Kasino	dass kasseeno
castle	das Schloss	dass shloss
cat	die Katze	dee kattser
catalogue	der Katalog	dayr kataloag
cathedral	die Kathedrale	dee kattee-drarler
cauliflower	der Blumenkohl/	dayr bloomen-koal
	der Karfiol (S. Ger/Aus)	dayr karfeeol
cave	die Höhle	dee hoehler
CD	die CD	dee tsaydee
celebrate	feiern	faiern
cellotape	das Klebeband	dass klayberbant
cemetery	der Friedhof	dayr freethoaf
centimetre	der/das Zentimeter	dayr/dass tsen-tee-mayter
central heating	die Zentralheizung	dee tsentrarl-hai-tsoong
centre	die Mitte	dee mitter
centre	das Zentrum	dass tsen troom
chair	der Stuhl	dayr shtool
chambermaid	das Zimmermädchen	dass tsimmer-maydkhen

champagne	der Champagner/Sekt	*dayr shampanyer/zekt*
change (alter)	ändern	*endern*
change (one thing for another)	wechseln	*vekhseln*
change (trains)	umsteigen	*oomshtaigen*
change the baby's nappy	wickeln	*vikkeln*
chapel	die Kapelle	*dee kappeller*
chat up	jemand anmachen/ sich jemand angeln	*yaymant anmakhen/ zikh yaymant angeln*
check	kontrollieren	*kontrolleeren*
check in	sich anmelden	*zikh anmelden*
cheers	Prost/zum Wohl	*prost/tsoom voal*
cheese (mature, mild)	der Käse(alte, junge)	*dayr kayzer (alter, yoonger)*
chef	der Chef	*dayr shef*
chemist	die Drogerie	*dee drogeree*
cheque	der Scheck	*dayr shek*
cherries	Kirschen	*dee keershen*
chess	das Schachspiel	*dass shakhshpeel*
chewing gum	der/das Kaugummi	*dayr/dass kowgoomee*
chicken	das Huhn/Hühnchen/ Hähnchen	*dass hoon/huenkhen/ haynkhen*
chicory	der Chicorée	*dayr chikoree*
child	das Kind	*dass kint*
child's seat	der Kindersitz	*dayr kinderzits*
chilled	gekühlt	*gekuehlt*
chin	das Kinn	*dass kinn*
chips	Pommes frites	*pomm frits*
chocolate	die Schokolade	*dee shoko-larder*
choose	wählen	*vaylen*
chop	das Kotelett	*dass kotlayt*
christian name	der Vorname	*dayr fornarmer*
church	die Kirche	*dee keerkher*
church service	der Gottesdienst	*dayr gottes-deenst*
cigar	die Zigarre	*dee tseegarrer*
cigar shop	der Tabakladen	*dayr tarbak-larden/*

cigarette	die Zigarette	*dee tseegaretter*
cigarette paper	das Zigarettenpapier	*dass tseegaretten-papeer*
ciné camera	die Filmkamera	*dee film-kamerar*
circle	der Kreis	*dayr krais*
circus	der Zirkus	*dayr tseerkooss*
city map	der Stadtplan	*dayr shtatplarn*
classical concert	das Klassikkonzert	*dass klasseek-kontsert*
clean	saubermachen	*zowber-makhen*
clean (vb.)	sauber	*zowber*
clear	deutlich	*doytlikh*
clearance	der Ausverkauf	*dayr owsfairkowf*
clock	die Uhr	*dee ooer*
closed	geschlossen	*geshlossen*
closed off	gesperrt	*geshpayrrt*
clothes	die Kleider	*dee klaider*
clothes hanger	der Kleiderbügel	*dayr klaider-buegel*
clothes peg	die Wäscheklammer	*dee vesher-klammer*
clothing (piece of)	das Kleidungsstück	*dass klaidoongs-shtook*
clothing	die Kleidung	*dee klaidoong*
coach	der Reisebus	*dayr raizerbooss*
coat	der Mantel	*dayr mantel*
cockroach	der Kakerlak	*dayr karkerlak*
cocoa	der Kakao	*dayr kakow*
cod	der Kabeljau	*dayr karbelyow*
coffee	der Kaffee	*dayr kaffay*
coffee filter	der Kaffeefilter	*dayr kaffay-filter*
cognac	der Kognak	*dayr konyak*
cold	kalt	*kalt*
cold (a)	die Erkältung	*dee ayrkeltoong*
cold cuts	der Aufschnitt	*dayr owfshnit*
collarbone	das Schlüsselbein	*dass shluessel-bain*
colleague	der Kollege	*dayr kolleger*
collision	der Zusammenstoss	*dayr tsoo-zammen-shtoas*
cologne	das Eau de toilette	*dass oadetwalet*
colour	die Farbe	*dee farber*
colour pencils	die Buntstifte	*dee boont-shtifter*
colouring book	das Malbuch	*dass marlbookh*

comb	der Kamm	*dayr kamm*
come	kommen	*kommen*
come back	zurückkommen	*tsooruek-kommen*
compartment	das Abteil	*dass aptail*
complaint (physical)	das Leiden	*dass laiden*
complaint	die Beschwerde/	*dee beshverder/*
	die Beanstandung	*dee bean-shtan-doong*
completely	ganz	*gants*
compliment	das Kompliment	*dass kompleement*
compulsory	verpflichtet	*fayrpflikhtet*
computer	Computer	*kompyootair*
concert	das Konzert	*dass kontsayrt*
concert hall	die Konzerthalle	*dee kontsayrt-haller*
concussion	die Gehirn-	*dee geheern-ayr-*
	erschütterung	*shuete-roong*
condensed milk	die Kaffeemilch/	*dee kaffay-milkh/*
	die Kondensmilch	*dee kondens-milkh*
condom	das Kondom/der	*dass kondoam/dayr*
	Pariser/das Gummi	*pareeser/dass goommee*
congratulate	gratulieren	*gratoo-leeren*
connection	die Verbindung	*dee fayr-bin-doong*
constipation	die Verstopfung	*dee fayr-shtop-foong*
consulate	das Konsulat	*dass konsoolart*
consultation	die Konsultation	*dee kon-sool-tat-tseeoan*
contact lens	die Kontaktlinse	*dee kontakt-linzer*
contact lens solution	das Kontaktlinsen mittel	*dass kontakt-linzen mittel*
contagious	ansteckend	*anshtekent*
contraceptive	das Verhütungsmittel	*dass fayr-hue-toongs-mittel*
contraceptive pill	die Verhütungspille	*dee fayr-hue-toongs-piller*
cook (verb)	kochen	*kokhen*
cook	der Koch	*dayr kokh*
copy	die Kopie	*dee kopee*
corkscrew	der Korkenzieher	*dayr korken-tseeher*
corn flour	das Maizena	*dass maitsenar*
corner	die Ecke	*dee ekker*
correct	korrekt	*korrekt*

correspond	korrespondieren	_korrespondeeren_
corridor	der Flur	_dayr flooer_
costume	der Anzug	_dayr antsook_
cot	das Kinderbett	_dass kinderbett_
cotton	die Baumwolle	_dee bowmvoller_
cotton wool	die Watte	_dee vatter_
cough	der Husten	_dayr hoosten_
cough mixture	der Hustensaft	_dayr hoostenzaft_
counter	der Schalter	_dayr shalter_
country	das Land	_dass lant_
country code	die Ländernummer	_dee lender-noommer_
courgette	die Zucchini	_dee tsookeenee_
course (medical)	die Kur	_dee koor_
cousin	der Cousin (m)/	_dayr koozeen/_
	die Cousine (f)	_dee koozeener_
crab	die Krabbe	_dee krabber_
cream	die Creme	_dee kraymer_
cream (for cooking)	die Sahne/der Rahm/	_dee zarner/dayr rarm_
credit card	die Kreditkarte	_dee kredeet-karter_
crisps	die Chips	_dee chips_
croissant	das Croissant/	_dass krwassan/_
	das Hörnchen	_dass hoernshen_
cross (the road)	überqueren	_ueber kvayren_
crossing	die Überfahrt	_dee ueberfart_
cry	weinen	_vainen_
cucumber	die (Salat)gurke	_dee (zalart)goorker_
cuddly toy	das Kuscheltier	_dass kooshelteer_
cuff links	die Manschetten knöpfe	_dee man-shetten-knoepfer_
cup	die Tasse	_dee tasser_
	die Schale (Aus.)	_dee sharler_
curly	lockig	_lokikh_
current	die Strömung	_dee shtroemoong_
cushion	das Kissen	_dass kissen_
customary	üblich	_ueblikh_
customs	der Zoll/die Zoll-	_dayr tsoll/dee tsol-_
	kontrolle	_kontroller_

cut	schneiden	*shnaiden*
cutlery	das Besteck	*dass beshtek*
cycle	fahrradfahren	*far-rart-fahren*

D

daily	jeden Tag	*yayden tark*
dairy products	Molkereiprodukte	*molkerai-prodookter*
damaged	beschädigt	*beshaydikt*
dance	tanzen	*tantsen*
danger	die Gefahr	*dee gefar*
dangerous	gefährlich	*gefayrlikh*
dark	dunkel	*doonkel*
date	die Verabredung	*dee fayr-ap-ray-doong*
daughter	die Tochter	*dee tokhter*
day	der Tag	*dayr tark*
day before yesterday	vorgestern	*forgestern*
dead	tot	*toat*
decaffeinated	koffeinfrei	*koffayeen-frai*
December	der Dezember	*dayr detsember*
deck chair	der Strandstuhl/	*dayr shtrantshtool/*
	Strandkorb	*dayr shtrantkorp*
declare (customs)	verzollen	*fayrtsollen*
deep	tief	*teef*
deepfreeze	einfrieren	*ainfreeren*
degrees	Grad	*grart*
delay	die Verspätung	*dee fayrshpaytoong*
delicious	vorzüglich	*fortsueglikh*
dentist	der Zahnarzt/	*dayr tsarnartst/*
	der Dentist	*der denteest*
dentures	das Kunstgebiss	*dass koonstgebiss*
deodorant	das Deo(dorant)	*dass deo(dorant)*
department	die Abteilung	*dee aptailoong*
department store	das Kaufhaus	*dass kowfhows*
departure	die Abfahrt/(flight)	*dee apfahrt/*
	der Abflug	*dayr apflook*

departure time	die Abfahrtszeit	*dee apfahrts-tsait*
depilatory cream	die Enthaarungs creme	*dee ent-hahroongs kraymer*
deposit (to)	zur Aufbewahrung (geben)	*tsoor owf-bevaroong (gayben)*
deposit	die Kaution	*dee kowtseeoan*
dessert	die Nachspeise	*dee nakhshpaizer*
destination	das (End)ziel	*dass (ent)tseel*
destination (mail)	der Bestimmungsort	*dayr be-shtimoongs-ort*
develop	entwickeln	*entvikkeln*
diabetic	der Diabetiker (m.)/ die Diabetikerin (f.)	*dayr deeearbayteeker/ dee deeearbayteekerin*
dial	wählen	*vaylen*
diamond	der Diamant	*dayr deeearmant*
diarrhoea	der Durchfall	*dayr doorkhfall*
dictionary	das Wörterbuch	*dass voerter-bookh*
diesel	der Diesel	*dayr deezel*
diet	die Diät	*dee deeyayt*
difficulty	die Schwierigkeit	*dee shveerikh-kait*
digital	digital	*digitarl*
dining room	der Speisesaal	*dayr shpaizerzaal*
dining/buffet car	der Speisewagen	*dayr shpaizer-vargen*
dinner (to have)	zu Abend essen	*tsoo arbent-essen*
dinner	das Abendessen	*dass arbentessen*
dinner jacket	der Smoking	*dayr smoking*
direction	die Richtung	*dee rikhtoong*
directly	direkt	*deerekt*
dirty	schmierig/schmutzig	*shmeerikh/shmootsikh*
disabled	der/die Behinderte	*dayr/dee-behin-dayrter*
disco	die Disko	*dee disko*
discount	die Ermässigung/ der Nachlass	*dee ermaysi-goong/ dayr nakhlass*
dish	das Gericht	*dass gerikht*
dish of the day	das Tagesgericht	*dass targes-gerikht*
disinfectant	das Desinfektions- mittel	*dass dez-infektseey oanzmittel*
distance	die Entfernung	*dee entfayr-noong*
distilled water	das destillierte Wasser	*dass destileerter-vasser*

disturb	stören	shtoeren
disturbance	die Störung	dee shtoeroong
dive	tauchen	towkhen
diving	der Tauchsport	dayr towkhshport
diving (deep sea)	das Tiefseetauchen	dass teefzaytowkhen
diving board	das Sprungbrett	dass shproongbret
diving gear	die Taucherausrüstung	dee towkher-owsruestoong
divorced	geschieden	gesheeden
DIY-shop	der Heimwerkermarkt	dayr haim-vayrker-markt
dizzy	schwind(e)lig	shvind(e)likh
do	tun	toon
doctor	der Arzt (m.)/	dayr artst/
	die Ärztin (f.)	dee ayrtstin
dog	der Hund	dayr hoont
doll	die Puppe	dee pupper
domestic	das Inland	dass inlant
done (cooked)	gar	gar
door	die Tür	dee tuer
double	Doppel-	doppel-
down	unten	oonten
draught	der Zug	dayr tsook
draughts	das Damespiel	dass darmeshpeel
dream	träumen	troymen
dress	das Kleid	dass klait
dressing gown	der Morgenmantel	dayr morgen-mantel
drink	trinken	trinken
drinking water	das Trinkwasser	dass-trinkvasser
drive	fahren	faren
driver	der Fahrer	dayr farer
driving licence	der Führerschein	dayr fuerershain
drought	die Trockenheit	dee trokkenhait
dry (vb.)	trocknen	trokknen
dry	trocken	trokken
dry clean	reinigen	rainigen
dry cleaner's	die Reinigung	dee rainigoong
dummy	der Schnuller	dayr shnooller

| during | während | *vayrent* |
| during the day | tagsüber | *targsueber* |

E

ear	das Ohr	*dass oa-er*
ear, nose and throat	der Hals-, Nasen-,	*dayr halz-, narzen-,*
(ENT) specialist	Ohrenarzt (HNO)	*oarenartst (har enn oh)*
earache	die Ohrenschmerzen	*dee oaren-shmairtsen*
eardrops	die Ohrentropfen	*dee oaren-tropfen*
early	früh	*frueh*
earrings	die Ohrringe	*dee oarringer*
earth	die Erde	*dee erder*
earthenware	die Keramik	*dee kayrarmik*
east	der Osten	*dayr osten*
easy	leicht/(comfortable)	*laikht/*
	bequem	*bekvaym*
eat	essen	*essen*
eczema	das Ekzem	*dass ektsaym*
eel	der Aal	*dayr arl*
egg	das Ei	*dass ai*
elastic band	das Gummi	*dass goomee*
electric	elektrisch	*elektrish*
electricity	der Strom	*dayr shtroam*
e-mail	e-Mail	*eemail*
embassy	die Botschaft	*dee boatshaft*
emergency brake	die Notbremse	*dee noat-bremzer*
emergency exit	der Notausgang	*dayr noat-owsgang*
emergency number	die Notrufnummer	*dee noat-roof-noommer*
emergency phone	die Notrufsäule	*dee noat-roof-zoyler*
emery board	die Nagelfeile	*dee nargelfailer*
empty	leer	*layr*
engaged	verlobt	*fayrloabt*
(to be married)		
engaged	besetzt	*bezetst*

England	England	*englant*
English	englisch	*english*
Englishman	der Engländer	*dayr englender*
Englishwoman	die Engländerin	*dee englenderin*
enjoy	genießen	*geneessen*
entertainment guide	der Veranstaltungs-kalender	*dayr fayr-anshtal-toongs kalender*
envelope	der Umschlag	*dayr umshlark*
evening	der Abend	*dayr arbent*
evening wear	die Abendkleidung	*dee arbent-klai-doong*
event	die Veranstaltung	*dee fair-an-shtal-toong*
every time	jedesmal	*yaydezmarl*
everything	alles	*alless*
everywhere	überall	*ueberarl*
examine	untersuchen	*oonter-zookhen*
excavation	die Ausgrabung	*dee owsgrarboong*
excellent	ausgezeichnet	*ows getsaikh-net*
exchange	(aus)tauschen	*(ows)towshen*
exchange office	das Wechselbüro	*dass vekhsel-buero*
exchange rate	der Wechselkurs	*dayr vekhselkoors*
excursion	der Ausflug	*dayr owsflook*
exhibition	die Ausstellung	*dee owsshteloong*
exit	der Ausgang	*dayr owsgang*
expenses	die Unkosten	*dee oonkosten*
expensive	teuer	*toyer*
explain	erklären	*ayrklayren*
express	der Schnellzug	*dayr shnelltsoog*
external	äusserlich	*oysserlikh*
eye	das Auge	*dass owger*
eyedrops	die Augentropfen	*dee owgentropfen*
eyeshadow	der Lidschatten	*dayr leetshatten*
eye specialist	der Augenarzt	*dayr owgenartst*
eyeliner	der Eyeliner	*dayr ailainer*

face	das Gesicht	*dass gezikht*
factory	die Fabrik	*dee fabreek*
fair	die Kirmes	*dee keermess*
fall	stürzen/fallen	*shtuertsen/fallen*
family	die Familie	*dee fameelier*
famous	berühmt	*beruemt*
far away	weit weg	*vait vek*
farm	der Bauernhof	*dayr bowernhoaf*
farmer	der Bauer	*dayr bower*
farmer's wife	die Bäuerin	*dee boyerin*
fashion	die Mode	*dee moader*
fast	schnell	*shnell*
father	der Vater	*dayr farter*
fault	die Schuld	*dee shoolt*
fax	telefaxen	*teleefaksen*
February	der Februar	*dayr febrooar/*
	der Feber (Aus.)	*dayr fayber*
feel	fühlen	*fuelen*
feel like	Lust haben	*loost harben*
fence	der Zaun	*dayr tsown*
ferry	die Fähre	*dee fayrer*
fever	das Fieber	*dass feeber*
fill	füllen	*fuelen*
fill out	ausfüllen	*owsfuellen*
filling	die Füllung	*dee fuelloong*
film	der Film	*dayr film*
filter	der/das Filter	*dayr/dass filter*
find	finden	*finden*
fine	der Strafzettel	*dayr shtrarftsettel*
finger	der Finger	*dayr finger*
fire	das Feuer	*das foyer*
fire brigade	die Feuerwehr	*dee foyer-vayr*
fire escape	die Feuertreppe	*dee foyer-trepper*
fire extinguisher	der Feuerlöscher	*dayr foyer-loesher*
first	erst/erste/erster	*ayrst/ayrster/ayrster*

first aid	die Erste Hilfe	dee ayrster-hilfer
first class	erster Klasse	ayrster klasser
fish (verb)	angeln	angeln
fish	der Fisch	dayr fish
fishing rod	die Angel	dee angel
fit	passen	passen
fitness centre	das Fitness-Zentrum	dass fitness-tsentroom
fitness training	das Fitness-Training	dass fitness-trayneeng
fitting room	die Anprobekabine	dee an-prober-kabeener
fix	flicken	flikken
flag	die Fahne/die Flagge	dee farner/dee flagger
flat	die Etagenwohnung	dee etarjen-voh-noong
flea market	der Flohmarkt	dayr flohmarkt
flight	der Flug	dayr flook
flight number	die Flugnummer	dee flooknoommer
flood	die Überschwemmung	dee ueber-shwem-moong
floor	der Stock/die Etage	dayr shtok/dee etarjer
flounder	die Flunder	dee floonder
flour	das Mehl	dass mayhl
flu	die Grippe	dee gripper
fly (insect)	die Fliege	dee fleeger
fly (verb)	fliegen	fleegen
fly-over	das Viadukt	dass fiadookt
fog	der Nebel	dayr naybel
foggy (to be)	neblig sein	nayblikh zain
folding caravan	der Faltwagen	dayr faltvargen
folkloristic	folkloristisch	folkloristish
follow	folgen	folgen
food	Lebensmittel	laybens-mittel
food poisoning	die Lebensmittel-vergiftung	dee laybenzmittel fairgif-toong
foot	der Fuss	dayr fooss

football	der Fussball	dayr fussball
football match	das Fussballspiel	dass fussball-shpeel
for	vor	for
forbidden	verboten	fairboaten
forehead	die Stirn	dee shtirn
foreign	ausländisch	owslendish
forget	vergessen	fairgessen
fork	die Gabel	dee garbel
form	das Formular	dass formoolar
fort	die Festung	dee festoong
forward	nachschicken	nakhshikken
fountain	der Springbrunnen	dayr shpring-broonnen
frame	das Gestell	dass geshtel
free	frei/gratis	frai/grartis
free time	die Freizeit	dee fraitsait
freeze	gefrieren	gefreeyeren
French	französisch	frantsoezish
French bread	das Stangenweiss brot/die Baguette	dass shtangenvaiss-broat/dee baguetter
fresh	frisch	frish
Friday	der Freitag	dayr fraitark
fried	gebacken	gebacken
fried egg	das Spiegelei	dass shpeegelai
friend	der Freund	dayr froynt
friendly	freundlich	froyntlikh
frightened	ängstlich	enkstlikh
fruit	das Obst	dass oapst
fruit juice	der Obstsaft	dayr oapst-zaft
frying pan	die (Brat)pfanne	dee (brart)pfanner
full	voll	foll
fun	das Vergnügen/ der Spass	dass fergnuegen/ dayr shpass

G

gallery	die Galerie	dee galleree-er
game	das Spiel(chen)	dass shpeel(khen)
garage	die Werkstatt	dee verkshtatt
garbage bag	der Müllsack	dayr muelzak
garden	der Garten	dayr garten
gas	das Campinggas	dass kamping-gas
(propane camping)	(das Propangas)	(dass proaparn-gas)
gastroenteritis	die Magen- und	dee margen- oont
	Darmbeschwerden	darmbeshvayrden
gate	das Tor	dass torr
gauze	der Verbandmull	dayr fayrbantmool
gear	der Gang	dayr gang
gel	das Gel	dass jel
German	deutsch	doytsh
Germany	Deutschland	doytshlant
get lost	sich verirren	zikh fayreeren
get married	heiraten	hai-rarten
get off	aussteigen	ows-shtaigen
gift	das Geschenk	dass geshenk
gilt	vergoldet	fairgoldet
ginger	der Ingwer	dayr ingver
girl	das Mädchen	dass maydkhen
girlfriend	die Freundin	dee froyndin
glacier	der Gletscher	dayr gletsher
glass	das Glas	dass glas
glasses (sun)	die Sonnenbrille	dee zonnen-briller
gliding	das Segelfliegen	dass zaygel-fleegen
glove	der Handschuh	dayr hantshoo
glue	der Klebstoff	dayr klaypshtoff
gnat	die Mücke	dee muekker
go (on foot)	gehen	gayhen
go back	zurückgehen/(car)	tsueruek-gayhen/
	zurückfahren	tsueruek-faren
go out	ausgehen	owsgayhen

goat's cheese	der Ziegenkäse	*dayr tseegen kayzer*
gold	das Gold	*dass golt*
golf	das Golfspiel	*dass golfshpeel*
golf course	der Golfplatz	*dayr golfplats*
gone	weg	*vek*
good day	guten Tag (Aus. servus) (Sw. Grüezi)	*gooten tark zairvoos gruetsee*
good evening	guten Abend	*gooten arbent*
good morning	guten Morgen	*gooten morgen*
good night	gute Nacht	*gooter nakht*
goodbye	auf Wiedersehen	*owf veederzayn*
government	regierung	*regeerung*
gram	das Gramm	*dass gramm*
grandchild	das Enkelkind	*dass enkel-kint*
grandfather	der Opa	*dayr oapa*
grandmother	die Oma	*dee oamar*
grape juice	der Traubensaft	*dayr trowbenzaft*
grapefruit	die Pampelmuse	*dee pampel-moozer*
grapes	die (Wein)trauben	*dee (vain)trowben*
grave	das Grab	*dass grarp*
grease	das Fett	*dass fett*
green	grün	*gruen*
green card	die grüne Karte	*dee gruener karter*
greet	begrüssen	*begruessen*
grey	grau	*grow*
grill	grillen	*grillen*
grilled	geröstet	*geroestet*
grocer	der Kaufmann/ Gemüsehändler	*dayr kowfmann/ gemueser haentler*
ground	der Boden	*dayr boaden*
group	die Gruppe	*dee grupper*
guest house	die Pension	*dee penseeoan*
guide (person/book)	der Führer	*dayr fuehrer*
guided tour	die Führung	*dee fueroong*
gynaecologist	der Frauenarzt	*dayr frowen-artst*

hair	das Haar	dass har
hairbrush	die Haarbürste	dee harbuerster
hairdresser	der Damen-, Herren- frisör	dayr darmen-, hayrren frizoer
hairspray	das Haarspray	dass harspray
hairdryer	föhn	foen
half	halb	halp
half (n.)	die Hälfte	dee helfter
half an hour	eine halbe Stunde	aine halpe shtoonder
half full	halb voll	halp foll
ham (boiled)	der Kochschinken	dayr kokh-shinken
ham (smoked)	der Räucherschinken	dayr roykher-shinken
hammer	der Hammer	dayr hammer
hand	die Hand	dee hant
handbrake	die Handbremse	dee hantbremzer
handbag	die Handtasche	dee hant-tasher
handkerchief	das Taschentuch	dass tashentookh
handmade	handgearbeitet	hant-ge-ar-bai-tet
happy	froh	fro
harbour	der Hafen	dayr harfen
hard	hart	hart
hat	der Hut	dayr hoot
hat (cap)	die Mütze	dee muetser
hayfever	der Heuschnupfen	dayr hoyshnoopfen
hazelnut	die Haselnuss	dee harzelnooss
head	der Kopf	dayr kopf
headache	die Kopfschmerzen	dee kopf-shmer-tsen
health	die Gesundheit	dee gezoonthait
health food shop	das Reformgeschäft	dass reform-gesheft
hear	hören	hoeren
hearing aid	das Hörgerät	dass hoergerayt
heart	das Herz	dass hayrts
heart patient	der Herzkranke	dayr hayrts-kranker
heater	die Heizung	dee haitsoong
heavy	schwer	shvayr

heel	die Ferse	*dee fayrzer*
heel (shoe)	der Absatz	*dayr apzats*
hello	Hallo	*hullo*
helmet	der Helm	*dayr helm*
help	helfen	*helfen*
help	die Hilfe	*dee hilfer*
helping	die Portion	*dee portseeyoan*
herbal tea	der Kräutertee	*dayr kroytertay*
herbs	die Gewürze/(green) die Kräuter	*dee gevuertser/ dee kroyter*
here	hier	*heer*
here you are	(giving sb sth) hier/ (on finding sb) da bist du ja!/(on finding sth) da ist es ja!	*heer/dar bist doo yar/ dar ist ez yar*
herring	der Hering	*dayr hayring*
high	hoch	*hokh*
high tide	die Flut	*dee floot*
highchair	der Kinderstuhl	*dayr kindershtool*
hiking	der Wandersport	*dayr vandershport*
hiking trip	die Wanderung	*dee vanderoong*
hip	die Hüfte	*dee huefter*
hire (for)	zu vermieten	*tsoo fairmeeten*
hire	mieten	*meeten*
hitchhike	per Anhalter fahren/ trampen	*payr anhalter faren/ trampen*
hobby	das Hobby	*dass hobby*
holiday	der Feiertag	*dayr fayertark*
holiday	die Ferien/der Urlaub	*dee fayreeyen/dayr oorlowp*
holiday house	die Ferienwohnung	*dee fayreeyen-voanoong*
holiday park	der Bungalowpark	*der bungaloapark*
homesickness	das Heimweh	*dass haimvay*
honest	ehrlich	*ayrlikh*
honey	der Honig	*dayr hoanikh*
horizontal	horizontal	*horeetsontarl*
horrible	scheusslich	*shoyslikh*
horse	das Pferd	*dass pfayrt*

hospital	das Krankenhaus (Aus.,Sw.) das Hospital/Spital	*dass krankenhowz dass hospitarl dass shpitarl*
hospitality	die Gastfreundschaft	*dee gast-froynt-shaft*
hot (spicy)	pikant	*peekant*
hot-water bottle	die Wärmflasche	*dee vayrm-flasher*
hotel	das Hotel	*dass hotel*
hour	die Stunde	*dee shtoonder*
house	das Haus	*dass howz*
household items	die Haushaltsartikel	*dee howz-halts-artee-kel*
Houses of Parliament	das Parlaments- gebäude	*dass parlaments geboyder*
housewife	die Hausfrau	*dee hows frow*
how far?	wie weit?	*vee vait?*
how long?	wie lange?	*vee langer?*
hungry (to be)	hungrig	*hoongrikh*
hurricane	der Orkan	*dayr orkarn*
hurry	die Eile	*dee ailer*
husband	der (Ehe) mann	*dayr (ayher) man*
hut (mountain)	die Berghütte	*dee bairghuetter*
hut	die Hütte	*dee huetter*
hyperventilation	die Hyperventilation	*dee hueper-ventee la-tseeoan*

I

ice cubes	die Eiswürfel	*dee aiz-vuer-fell*
ice skating	das Schlittschuhlaufen	*dass shlit-shoo-lowfen*
ice-cream	das (Speise)eis	*dass shpaizeraiz*
idea	die Idee	*dee eeday*
identification	der Ausweis	*dayr owsvaiss*
identify	identifizieren	*eedentee-fi-tsee-ren*
ill	krank	*krank*
illness	die Krankheit	*dee krankhait*
imagination	die Vorstellung	*dee forshtelloong*
immediately	sofort	*zofort*

import duty	Einfuhrzölle	*ainfoor-tsoeller*
impossible	unmöglich	*oonmoeglikh*
in	in	*in*
in the evening	abends	*arbents*
in the morning	morgens	*morgens*
included	enthalten/	*enthalten/*
	einschliesslich	*ainshleesslikh*
indicate	zeigen	*tsaigen*
indicator	der Blinker	*dayr blinker*
industrial art	das Kunstgewerbe	*dass koonstgewayrber*
inexpensive	billig	*billikh*
infection	die Virusinfektion,	*dee veeroos-infekts*
(viral, bacterial)	die bakterielle	*eeoan, dee bakteereey*
	Infektion	*eller infektseeoan*
inflammation	die Entzündung	*dee ent-tsuen-doong*
information	die Angaben/	*dee angarben/ dee*
	die Auskunft	*owskunft*
information office	das Auskunftsbüro	*dass ows-kunfts-bueroh*
injection	die Spritze	*dee shpritser*
injured	verletzt	*fayrletst*
innocent	unschuldig	*oonshooldikh*
insect	das Insekt	*dass inzekt*
insect bite	der Insektenstich	*dayr inzekten-shtikh*
insect repellent	das Mückenöl	*dass muekkenoel*
inside	drin(nen)	*drin(nen)*
insole	die Einlegesohle	*dee ainlaygesohler*
instructions	die Gebrauchs-	*dee gebrowkhs-*
	anweisung	*anvai zoong*
insurance	die Versicherung	*dee fayrzikheroong*
intermission	die Pause	*dee powzer*
international	international	*eenter-natseeoa-narl*
interpreter	der Dolmetscher	*dayr dolmetsher*
intersection	die Kreuzung	*dee kroytsoong*
introduce oneself	sich vorstellen	*sikh forshtellen*
invite	einladen	*ainlarden*
iodine	das Jod	*dass yot*
Ireland	Irland	*eerlant*

Irish	irländisch	*eerlendish*
Irishman	der Ire	*dayr eerer*
Irishwoman	die Irin	*dee eerin*
iron (vb.)	bügeln	*byoogelln*
iron	das Bügeleisen	*dass buegell-aizen*
ironing board	das Bügelbrett	*dass buegelbrett*
island	die Insel	*dee inzel*
Italian	italienisch	*italeeaynish*
Italy	Italien	*itarlee-en*
itch	das Jucken	*dass yooken*

J

jack	der Wagenheber	*dayr vargen-hayber*
jacket	die Jacke	*dee yakker*
jam	die Marmelade	*dee marmelarder*
January	der Januar/	*dayr yanooar/*
	der Jenner (Aus.)	*dayr yenner*
jaw	der Kiefer	*dayr keefer*
jellyfish	die Qualle	*dee kvaller*
jeweller	der Juwelier	*dayr yoovayleer*
jewellery	der Schmuck	*dayr shmook*
jog	joggen	*joggen*
joke	der Witz	*dayr vits*
juice	der Saft	*dayr zaft*
July	der Juli	*dayr yoolee*
jump leads	das Startkabel	*dass shtartkarbel*
jumper	der Pullover	*dayr pullover*
June	der Juni	*dayr yooni*

K

key (ignition)	der Zündschlüssel	*dayr tsuent-shluessel*
key	der Schlüssel	*dayr shluessel*
kilo	das Kilo	*dass keelo*
kilometre	der Kilometer	*dayr keelo-mayter*
king	der König	*dayr koenikh*
kiss (vb.)	küssen	*kuessen*
kiss	der Kuss	*dayr kooss*
kitchen	die Küche	*dee kuekher*
knee	das Knie	*dass knee*
knife	das Messer	*dass messer*
knit	stricken	*shtrikken*
know	wissen	*vissen*

L

lace	der Schnürsenkel	*dayr shnuerzenkel*
ladies toilet	die Damentoilette	*dee darmen-twalet-ter*
lake	der See	*dayr zay*
lamp	die Lampe	*dee lamper*
land	landen	*landen*
lane	die Fahrspur	*dee fahrshpoor*
language	die Sprache	*dee shprakher*
large	gross	*groass*
last	letzte	*letster*
late	spät	*shpayt*
later	nachher	*nakh her*
laugh	lachen	*lakhen*
launderette	die Münzwäscherei	*dee muents-vesheray*
law	das Recht	*dass rekht*
laxative	das Abführmittel	*dass ap-fuer-mittel*
leaded (petrol)	das Super(benzin)	*dass zooper(bentseen)*
leak	das Loch	*dass lokh*
leather	das Leder	*dass layder*
leather goods	Lederwaren	*layder varen*

leave	abfahren/abfliegen	*apfahren/apfleegen*
leek	der Porree/der Lauch	*dayr porray/dayr lowkh*
left	links	*links*
left	nach links	*nakh links*
leg	das Bein	*dass bain*
lemon	die Zitrone	*dee tsitroner*
lemonade	die Limonade	*dee limonarder*
lend	leihen	*laihen*
lens	die Linse	*dee linzer*
lentils	die Linsen	*dee linzen*
less	weniger	*vayniger*
lesson	die Stunde	*dee shtoonder*
letter	der Brief	*dayr breef*
lettuce	der Kopfsalat	*dayr kopfzalart*
level crossing	der Bahnübergang	*dayr barn-ueber-gang*
library	die Bibliothek	*dee beebleeotayk*
lie (tell lie)	lügen	*luegen*
lie	liegen	*leegen*
lift (hitchhike)	die Mitfahr gelegenheit	*dee mit-far-gelaygenhait*
lift (in building)	der Fahrstuhl/der Aufzug	*dayr farshtool/ der owftsook*
lift (ski)	der (Sessel)lift	*dayr (zessel)lift*
light (colour)	hell	*hell*
light (weight)	leicht	*laikht*
lighter	das Feuerzeug	*dass foyer-tsoyk*
lighthouse	der Leuchtturm	*dayr loykht toorm*
lightning	der Blitz	*dayr blits*
like	mögen/lieben (stronger)	*moergen/leeben*
line	die Linie	*dee leenier*
linen	das Leinen	*dass lainen*
lipstick	der Lippenstift	*dayr lippen-shtift*
liqueur	der Likör	*dayr leekoer*
liquorice	die Lakritze(n)	*dee lakritzer(n)*
listen	(zu)hören	*(tsoo)hoeren*
literature	die Literatur	*dee literatoor*
litre	der/das Liter	*dayr/dass leeter*

little	wenig	*vaynikh*
little (a)	das bisschen, ein bisschen	*dass bis-shen, ain bis-shen*
live	wohnen	*voanen*
live together	zusammenleben	*tsoo-zammen-layben*
lobster	der Hummer	*dayr hoommer*
local	örtlich	*oertlikh*
lock	das Schloss	*dass shloss*
locker (luggage)	das Schliessfach (für Gepäck)	*dass shleesfakh (fuer gepek)*
long	lang	*lang*
look	schauen	*showern*
look for	suchen	*zookhen*
look up	aufsuchen	*owfzookhen*
lorry	der LKW/der Last- wagen	*dayr ellkarvay/ dayr lasstvargen*
lose	verlieren	*fayrleeren*
loss	der Verlust	*dayr fayrloost*
lost	weg/vermisst (also people)	*vek/fayrmisst*
lost	verloren	*fayrloren*
lost property office	das Fundbüro	*dass foontbuero*
lotion	die Lotion	*dee loatseeoan*
loud	laut	*lowt*
love (vb.)	sich lieben	*zikh leeben*
love	die Liebe	*dee leeber*
low	niedrig	*needrikh*
low tide	die Ebbe	*dee ebber*
luck	das Glück	*dass gluek*
luggage (left)	die Gepäck- aufbewahrung	*dee gepek- owfbevaroong*
luggage	das Gepäck	*dass gepek*
luggage locker	das Schliessfach	*dass shleesfakh*
lumps (sugar)	die Zuckerwürfel	*dee tsooker-wuerfel*
lunch	das Mittagessen	*dass mittark-essen*
lungs	die Lungen	*dee loongen*

macaroni	Makkaroni	makaroanee
machine (vending)	der Automat	dayr owtomart
madam	meine Dame	mainer darmer
magazine	die Zeitschrift	dee tsaitshrift
mail	die Post	dee post
make an appointment	einen Termin machen	ainen tairmeen makhen
makeshift	provisorisch	proveezorish
manager	der Verwalter	dayr fayrvalter
manicure	die Maniküre	dee manee-kuerer
map	die (Land)karte	dee (lant)karter
marble	der Marmor	dayr marmor
March	der März	dayr mayrts
marina	der Yachthafen	dayr yakht harfen
market	der Markt	dayr markt
marriage	die Ehe	dee ayher
married	verheiratet	fayrhai-rartet
mass	die Messe	dee messer
massage	die Massage	dee massarjer
match	der Wettkampf	dayr vetkampf
matches	die Streichhölzer	dee shtraikh-hoeltser
May	der Mai	dayr mai
maybe	vielleicht	feelaikht
mayonnaise	die Mayonnaise	dee mayonnayzer
mayor	der Bürgermeister	dayr buerger-maister
meal	die Mahlzeit	dee marltsait
mean	bedeuten	bedoyten
meat	das Fleisch	dass flaish
medication	das Heilmittel	dass hailmittel
medicine	das Medikament	dass medee-kar-ment
meet	kennenlernen	kennen-layrnen
melon	die Melone	dee melowner
membership	die Mitgliedschaft	dee mitt-gleet-shaft
menstruate	(meine/ihre) Tage haben	(mainer/eerer) targer harben

menstruation	die Periode	*dee peereeoader*
menu	das Menü	*dass menue*
menu	die Speisekarte	*dee shpaizer-karter*
menu of the day	das Tagesmenü	*dass targez-menue*
message	der Bescheid/die Nachricht	*dayr beshait/dee nakhrikht*
metal	das Metall	*dass mettarl*
meter	der/das Taxameter	*dayr/dass taksamayter*
metre	der/das Meter	*dayr/dass mayter*
migraine	die Migräne	*dee meegrayner*
mild (tobacco)	(der) leicht(e) (Tabak)	*(dayr) laikht(er) (tarbak)*
milk	die Milch	*dee milkh*
millimetre	der/das Millimeter	*dayr/dass millimayter*
milometer	der Kilometerzähler	*dayr keelo-mayter-tsayler*
mince	das Mett/das Hackfleisch	*dass met/ dass hackflaish*
mineral water	das Mineralwasser	*dass minerarl vasser*
minute	die Minute	*dee meenooter*
mirror	der Spiegel	*dayr shpeegell*
miss	vermissen	*fayrmissen*
missing (to be)	fehlen	*faylen*
missing person	vermisste Person	*fayrmisster payrzoan*
mistake	der Fehler/der Irrtum	*dayr fayler/dayr eertoom*
mistaken (to be)	sich irren	*zikh irren*
misunderstanding	das Missverständnis	*dass miss-fayr-shtant-nis*
mocha	der Mokka	*dayr mokker*
modern art	die moderne Kunst	*dee moderner-koonst*
molar	der Backenzahn	*dayr bakkentsarn*
moment	der Augenblick	*dayr owgenblik*
moment	der Moment	*dayr moament*
monastery	das Kloster	*dass kloaster*
Monday	der Montag	*dayr moantark*
money	das Geld	*dass gelt*
month	der Monat	*dayr moanart*
moped	das Moped	*dass moaped*
mosque	die Moschee	*dee moshay*
motel	das Motel	*dass moatell*

mother	die Mutter	dee mooter
moto-cross	das Moto-Cross	dass moto-kross
motorbike	das Motorrad	dass moatorrart
motorboat	das Motorboot	dass moatorboat
motorway	die Autobahn	dee owtobarn
mountain	der Berg	dayr bayrk
mountaineering	der Bergsport	dayr bayrk-shporrt
mouse	die Maus	dee mows
mouth	der Mund	dayr munt
much/many	viel	feel
muscle	der Muskel	dayr mooskel
muscle spasms	die Muskelkrämpfe	dee mooskel-krempfer
museum	das Museum	dass moozayoom
mushrooms	die Pilze	dee piltser
music	die Musik	dee moozeek
musical	das Musical	dass moozeekall
mussels	die Muscheln	dee moosheln
mustard	der Senf/der Mostrich	dayr zenf/dayr mosstrikh

N

nail	der Nagel	dayr nargel
nail polish	der Nagellack	dayr nargellack
nail polish remover	der Nagellack entferner	nargel lack entfair-ner
nail scissors	die Nagelschere	dee nargelsheerer
naked	nackt	nakt
nappy	die Windel	dee vindel
nationality	die Staatsangehörig- gehoerig kait	dee shtarts-an-gehoerig- keit
natural	natürlich	natuerlikh
nature	die Natur	dee natoor
naturism	die Freikörperkultur	dee fray-koerper-kooltoor
nauseous	übel	uebel
near	bei	bai
nearby	in der Nähe	in dayr nayher
necessary	nötig/notwendig	noetikh/noatvendikh

neck	der Nacken	*dayr nakken*
necklace	die Kette	*dee ketter*
needle	die Nadel	*dee nardel*
negative	das Negativ	*dass negateef*
neighbours	die Nachbarn	*dee nakhbarn*
nephew	der Neffe	*dayr neffer*
never	nie	*nee*
new	neu	*noy*
news	die Nachricht	*dee nakh-rikht*
news-stand	der Kiosk	*dayr keeosk*
newspaper	die Zeitung	*dee tsaitoong*
next	nächste(r)	*nekhste(r)*
next to	neben	*nayben*
nice (friendly)/nice (to the eye)	nett/hübsch	*nett/huepsh*
nice (cosy)	gemütlich	*gemuetlikh*
nice (delicious)	lecker	*lekker*
niece	die Nichte	*dee nikhter*
night	die Nacht	*dee nakht*
night (at)	nachts	*nakhts*
night duty	der Nachtdienst	*dayr nakhtdeenst*
nightclub	der Nachtklub	*dayr nakhtkloop*
nightlife	das Nachtleben	*dass nakhtlayben*
no	nein	*nain*
no overtaking	das Überholverbot	*dass ueber-hoal-fayr-boat*
noise	der Lärm	*dayr layrm*
nonstop	nonstop	*nonstop*
no-one	niemand/keiner	*neemant/kainer*
normal	gewöhnlich	*gevoehnlikh*
north	der Norden	*der norden*
normal	normal	*normarl*
north	nördlich	*noerdlikh*
nose	die Nase	*dee narzer*
nose drops	Nasentropfen	*narzen-tropfen*
nosebleed	das Nasenbluten	*dass narzen-blooten*
notepaper	das Briefpapier	*dass breefpapeer*
nothing	nichts	*nikhts*

November	der November	*dayr november*
nowhere	nirgendwo	*neergentvo*
nude beach	der Nackt(bade)strand	*dayr nakt(barderr)shtrant*
number	die Nummer	*dee noommer*
number (subscriber's)	die Rufnummer	*dee roof-noommer*
number plate	das Nummernschild	*dass noommern-shilt*
nurse	die (Kranken)schwester	*dee (kranken)-shvester*
nutmeg	die Muskatnuss	*dee mooskartnooss*
nuts	die Nüsse	*dee nuesser*

O

October	der Oktober	*dayr oktoaber*
off (food)	verdorben	*fairdorben*
offer	anbieten	*anbeeten*
office	das Büro	*dass buero*
off-licence	der Spirituosen händler	*dayr shpiri-too-oazen-hendler*
oil (diesel)	das Dieselöl	*dass deezeloel*
oil	das Öl	*dass oel*
oil change	der Ölwechsel	*dayr oelvekhsel*
oil level	der Ölstand	*dayr oelshtant*
ointment	die Salbe	*dee zalber*
okay	einverstanden	*ain-fayr-shtanden*
old	alt	*alt*
olive oil	das Olivenöl	*dass oleevenoel*
olives	die Oliven	*dee oleeven*
omelette	das Omelett	*dass ommlett*
on	auf	*owf*
on the right	rechts	*rekhts*
on the way	unterwegs	*oontervaygs*
oncoming traffic	der Gegenverkehr	*dayr gaygen-fayrkayr*
one-way-traffic	der Einbahnverkehr	*dayr ain-barn-fayrkayr*
onion	die Zwiebel	*dee tsveebel*
open	öffnen	*oeffnen*

open	offen	*offen*
opera	die Oper	*dee oaper*
operate	operieren	*opereeren*
operator (telephone)	der Telefonist (m.)/ die Telefonistin (f.)	*der telefoanist/ dee telefoanistin*
operetta	die Operette	*dee operetter*
opposite	gegenüber	*gaygenueber*
optician	der Optiker	*dayr optiker*
or	oder	*oader*
orange	die Apfelsine/die Orange	*dee apfel-zeener/ dee oranje*
orange juice	der Orangensaft	*dayr oranjenzaft*
order	die Bestellung	*dee beshtelloong*
order (in), tidy	in Ordnung	*in ordnoong*
order	bestellen	*beshtellen*
other	andere/-s	*anderer/-s*
other side	die andere Seite	*dee anderer zaiter*
outside	(dr)aussen/raus (outwards)	*(dr)owssen, rows*
overtake	überholen (overtake) einholen (catch up)	*ueber-hoalen/ ainhoalen*
oysters	die Austern	*dee owstern*

P

packed lunch	das Lunchpaket	*dass loonch-pakayt*
pad (writing)	der Schreibblock (squared, lined)	*dayr shraipblok*
page	die Seite	*dee zaiter*
pain	der Schmerz, Schmerzen (pl.)	*dayr shmayrts, shmayrtsen*
painkiller	das Schmerzmittel	*dass shmayrts-mittel*
paint	die Farbe	*dee farber*
painting (art)	die Malerei	*dee marlerai*
painting (object)	das Gemälde	*dass gemelder*
palace	der Palast	*dayr palast*

pan	der Topf	dayr topf
pancake	der Eierkuchen/	dayr aierkookhen/
	der Pfannkuchen	dayr pfann-kookhen
pane	die Scheibe	dee shayber
panties	der Slip	dayr slip
pants	die Unterhose(n)	dee oonterhoaze(n)
panty liner	die Slipeinlage	dee shlip-ain-larger
paper	das Papier	dass papeer
paper (writing)	das Schreibpapier	dass shraip-papeer
paprika	der Paprika	dayr papreeker
paraffin oil	das Petroleum	dass petrolayoom
parasol	der Sonnenschirm	dayr zonnensheerm
parcel	das Paket/das	dass pakayt/dass
	Päckchen	pekshen
pardon	die Entschuldigung/	dee entshool-dee-
	die Verzeihung	goong/dee fayrtsayoong
parents	die Eltern	dee elltern
park	der Park	dayr park
park (car)	parken/parkieren (Sw.)	parken/parkeeren
parking space	der Parkplatz	dayr parkplats
parsley	die Petersilie	dee payterzeelier
part	das (Ersatz)teil	dass (ayrzats)tail
partition	die Trennwand	dee trennwant
partner	der Partner	dayr partner
party	das Fest/die Party	dass fest/dee party
passable	begehbar/	begaybar,
	befahrbar (vehicle)	befarbar
passenger	der Passagier	dayr passajeer
passport	der (Reise)pass	dayr (raizer)parss
passport photo	das Passbild	dass passbilt
patient	der Patient	dayr patseeyent
pavement	der Gehsteig/	dayr gayshtaik/
	das Trottoir	dass trottwar
pay	(be)zahlen	(be)tsarlen
pay the bill	abrechnen	aprekhnen
peach	der Pfirsich	dayr pfeerzikh
peanuts	die Erdnüsse	dee ertnuesser

pear	die Birne	*dee beerner*
peas	die Erbsen	*dee airpsen*
pedal	das Pedal	*dass pedarl*
pedicure	die Fusspflege	*dee fusspflayger*
pen	der Stift	*dayr shtift*
pencil	der Bleistift	*dayr blaishtift*
penis	der Penis	*dayr payniss*
pension	die Pension	*dee ponseeyoan*
pepper	der Pfeffer	*dayr pfeffer*
performance	die Theatervorstellung	*dee tayartter-for-shtelloong*
perfume	das Parfüm	*dass parfuem*
perm (to have a)	eine Dauerwelle machen	*einer dowerveller makhen*
perm	die Dauerwelle	*dee dowerveller*
permit	die Genehmigung/ die Erlaubnis	*dee genay-migoong/ dee erlowpniss*
person	die Person	*dee payrzoan*
personal	persönlich	*payrzoenlikh*
petrol	das Benzin	*dass bentseen*
petrol station	die Tankstelle	*dee tank-shteller*
pets	die Haustiere	*dee howz-teerer*
pharmacy	die Apotheke	*dee appotayker*
phone (tele-)	das Telefon	*dass talayfoan*
phone	telefonieren	*taylayfoaneeren*
phone box	die Telefonzelle	*dee taylayfoan-tseller*
phone charger (mobile)	Handyaufladegerät	*hendee-owf-lardegerayt*
phone directory	das Telefonbuch	*dass taylayfoan-bookh*
phone number	die Telefonnummer	*dee taylayfown-noomer*
photo	das Foto	*dass foto*
photocopier	das Kopiergerät	*dass kopee-gerayt*
photocopy (vb.)	fotokopieren	*foto-kopeeren*
photocopy	die Fotokopie	*dee fotokopee*
pick up (an object)	aufheben	*owfhayben*
pick up	(ab)holen	*(ap)hoalen*
picnic	das Picknick	*dass piknik*
pier	die Landungsbrücke	*dee landoongz-brueker*

pigeon	die Taube	*dee towber*
pill (contraceptive)	die Pille	*dee piller*
pill (morning-after)	die Pille danach	*dee piller danakh*
pillow	das Kissen	*dass kissen*
pillowcase	der Kissenüberzug	*dayr kissen-ueber-tsook*
pin	die Stecknadel	*dee shteknardel*
pineapple	die Ananas	*dee anarnass*
pipe	die Pfeife	*dee pfaifer*
pipe tobacco	der Pfeifentabak	*dayr pfaifen-tarbak*
pity	schade	*sharder*
place of interest	die Sehenswürdigkeit	*dee zayenz-vuerdeekh-kait*
plan	der Plan	*dayr plarn*
plant	die Pflanze	*dee pflantser*
plasters	das (Heft)pflaster	*dass (heft)pflaster*
plastic	das Plastik	*dass plastik*
plastic bag	die Tüte	*dee tueter*
plate	der Teller	*dayr teller*
platform	das Gleis	*dass glais*
platform	der Bahnsteig	*dayr barnshtaik*
play (theatre)	das Theaterstück	*dass tayarter-shtuek*
play	spielen	*shpeelen*
playground	der Spielplatz	*dayr shpeelplats*
playing cards	die Spielkarten	*dee shpeelkarten*
pleasant	angenehm	*angenaym*
please	bitte	*bitter*
pleasure	das Vergnügen	*dass fairgnuegen*
plum	die Pflaume	*dee pflowmer*
pocketknife	das Taschenmesser	*dass tashen-messer*
point	zeigen	*tsaigen*
poison	das Gift	*dass gift*
police	die Polizei	*dee poleetsai*
police station	die Polizeiwache	*dee poleetsai-vakher*
policeman	der Polizist	*dayr poleetsist*
pond	der Teich	*dayr taikh*
pony	das Pony	*dass poanee*
pop concert	das Popkonzert	*dass pop-kontsert*
population	die Bevölkerung	*dee befoelke-roong*

pork	das Schweinefleisch	*dass shvainerflaish*
port	der Port(wein)	*dayr port(vain)*
porter	der Gepäckträger/	*dayr gepek-trayger*
	der Pförtner	*dayr pfoertner*
post code	die Postleitzahl	*dee post-lait-tsarl*
post office	das Postamt	*dass postamt*
post office (main)	die Hauptpost	*dee howptpost*
postage	das Porto	*dass porto*
postbox	der Briefkasten	*dayr breef-kasten*
postcard	die Ansichtskarte/	*dee ansikhts-karter/*
	die Postkarte	*dee post-karter*
postman	der Briefträger	*dayr breeftrayger*
potato	die Kartoffel/	*dee kartoffell*
	die Heurigen (Aus.)	*dee hoyrigen*
poultry	das Geflügel	*dass gefluegel*
pound	das Pfund	*dass pfoont*
powdered milk	das Milchpulver	*dass milkh-pulver*
power point	der Elektroanschluss	*dayr elektro-anshluss*
pram	der Kinderwagen	*dayr kinder-vargen*
prawns	die Garnelen	*dee garnaylen*
precious	lieb/teuer	*leep/toyer*
prefer	vorziehen	*fortseehen*
preference	die Vorliebe	*dee forleeber*
pregnant	schwanger/in	*shvanger/in anderen*
	anderen Umständen	*oomshtenden*
present	vorhanden/	*forhanden/*
	anwesend (person)	*anvayzent*
present (gift)	das Geschenk	*dass geshenk*
press	drücken	*druekken*
pressure	der Druck	*dayr drook*
price	der Preis	*dayr praiss*
price list	die Preisliste	*dee praisslister*
print (vb.)	abziehen	*aptseehen*
print	der Abzug	*dayr aptsook*
probably	wahrscheinlich	*varshainlikh*
problem	das Problem	*dass problaym*
profession	der Beruf	*dayr beroof*

programme	das Programm	*dass programm*
pronounce	aussprechen	*owsshprekhen*
pub	die Kneipe	*dee knaiper*
pudding	der Pudding	*dayr pudding*
pull	ziehen	*tseehen*
pull a muscle	sich einen Muskel verzerren	*zikh ainen mooskel fayrtserren*
pure	pur	*poor*
purple	lila	*leelar*
purse	der Geldbeutel/das Portemonnaie/die Börse	*dayr geltboytel/ dass portmonnay/dee boerzer*
push	schieben/drücken	*sheeben/drueken*
puzzle	das Puzzle	*dass puzzle (pootsel)*
pyjamas	der Pyjama	*dayr peejarmar*

Q

quarter	das Viertel	*dass feartell*
quarter of an hour	die Viertelstunde	*dee fear-tell-shtoonder*
queen	die Königin	*dee koenigin*
question	die Frage	*dee frarger*
quick	schnell	*shnell*
quiet	ruhig	*roohikh*

R

radio	das Radio	*dass rardio*
railway	die (Bundes)bahn	*dee (boondez)barn*
rain	der Regen	*dayr raygen*
rain (verb)	regnen	*raygnen*
raincoat	der Regenmantel	*dayr raygenmantel*
raisins	die Rosinen	*dee rozeenen*
rape	die Vergewaltigung	*dee fair-gevalti-goong*
rapids	die Stromschnelle(n)	*dee shtroamshneller(n)*

rash	der Ausschlag	*dayr owsshlark*
raspberries	die Himbeeren	*dee himbeeren*
raw	roh	*roa*
raw vegetables	die Rohkost	*dee roakost*
razor blades	die Rasierklingen	*dee razeer-klingen*
read	lesen	*layzen*
ready	fertig	*fairtikh*
really	eigentlich	*aigentlikh*
receipt (written)	der Empfangsschein	*dayr empfangs-shain*
receipt (till-chit)	der Kassenzettel/die Quittung	*dayr kassentsettel/dee kvittoong*
recipe	das Rezept	*dass retsept*
reclining chair	der Liegestuhl	*dayr leegershtool*
recommend	empfehlen	*empfaylen*
recovery service	die Pannenhilfe	*dee pannen-hilfer*
rectangle	das Rechteck	*dass rekhtekk*
red	rot	*roat*
red wine	der Rotwein	*dayr roatvain*
reduction	die Ermässigung	*dee ermayssigoong*
refrigerator	der Kühlschrank	*dayr kuelshrank*
region	die Gegend	*dee gaygent*
registration	der Kraftfahrzeugschein	*dayr kraft-far-tsoyk-shain*
relatives	die Verwandten	*dee fayrvanten*
reliable	zuverlässig	*tsoofayrlessikh*
religion	der Glaube(n)/die Religion	*dayr glowber(n)/die religioan*
rent out	vermieten	*fayrmeeten*
repair	reparieren	*repareeren*
repairs	die Reparatur	*dee reparatoor*
repeat	wiederholen	*veederhoalen*
report	die Anzeige	*dee antsaiger*
reset	zurücksetzen	*tsooruek-zetsen*
responsible	verantwortlich	*fayr-antvort-likh*
rest	ausruhen	*owsroohen*
restaurant	das Restaurant	*dass restorant*
result	das Ergebnis	*dass ergaypniss*
retired	pensioniert	*penzeeo neert*

return (ticket)	die Rückfahrkarte	*dee rueck-far-karter*
reverse (vehicle)	rückwärts fahren	*ruekverts faren*
rheumatism	das Rheuma	*dass roymar*
rice	der Reis	*dayr raiss*
ridiculous	unsinnig	*oonzinnikh*
riding (horseback)	das Reiten	*dass raiten*
riding school	die Reitschule	*dee raitshooler*
right	rechts	*rekhts*
right of way	die Vorfahrt	*dee forfart*
ripe	reif	*raif*
risk	das Risiko	*dass reezeeko*
river	der Fluss	*dayr flooss*
road	der Weg	*dayr vayk*
roadway	die Fahrbahn	*dee farbarn*
roasted	gebraten	*gebrarten*
rock	der Fels(en)	*dayr felz(en)*
roll	das Brötchen/	*dass broetshen/*
	die Semmel,	*dee zemmel,*
	der Weck(en)	*dayr vekk(en)*
	(S.Ger.,Aus.)	
rolling tobacco	der Shag	*dayr shag*
roof rack	der Gepäckträger	*dayr gepek-trayger*
room	das Zimmer	*dass tsimmer*
room number	die Zimmernummer	*dee tsimmer-noommer*
room service	der Zimmerservice	*dayr tsimmer-zair-viss*
rope	das Seil	*dass zail*
rose	die Rose	*dee roazer*
rosé	rosa	*roaza*
roundabout	der Kreisverkehr/der	*dayr krays-fayr-kayr/*
	Kreisel	*dayr kraizel*
route	die Route	*dee rooter*
rowing boat	das Ruderboot	*dass rooderboat*
rubber	der/das Gummi	*dayr/dass goommee*
rubbish	der Quatsch	*dayr kvatsh*
rucksack	der Rucksack	*dayr rookzak*
rude	unhöflich	*oonhoeflikh*
ruins	die Ruinen	*dee rooeenen*

run (cross-country) die Langlaufloipe *dee lang-lowf-loyper*
run into treffen *treffen*

S

sad	traurig	*trowrikh*
safari	die Safari	*dee zafaree*
safe	sicher	*zikher*
safe	das Safe	*dass sayf*
safety pin	die Sicherheitsnadel	*dee zikher-haits-nardel*
sail	segeln	*zaygeln*
sailing boat	das Segelboot	*dass zaygelboat*
salad	der Salat	*dayr zalart*
salad oil	das Salatöl	*dass zalartoel*
sale	der Ausverkauf	*dayr owsferkowf*
salt	das Salz	*dass zalts*
same	der-/die-/dasselbe	*dayr-/dee-/dasszelber*
sandy beach	der Sandstrand	*dayr zantshtrant*
sanitary pad	die Damenbinde	*dee darmen-binder*
sardines	die Sardinen	*dee zardeenen*
satellite television	Satellitenfernsehen	*sutelitenfairnsayhen*
satisfied	zufrieden	*tsoofreeden*
Saturday	der Samstag/der	*dayr zamstark/*
	Sonnabend	*zonnarbent*
sauce	die Sosse	*dee zoaser*
sauna	die Sauna	*dee zowner*
sausage	die Wurst	*dee voorst*
savoury	herzhaft	*hayrts haft*
say	sagen	*zargen*
scarf	der Schal	*dayr sharl*
scenic walk	der Wanderweg	*dayr vandervayk*
school	die Schule	*dee shooler*
scissors	die Schere	*dee sheerer*
scooter	der Motorroller	*dayr moatoar-roller*
Scotland	Schottland	*shottlant*
Scotsman	der Schotte	*dayr shotter*

Scotswoman	die Schottin	*dee shottin*
Scottish	schottish	*shottish*
scrambled eggs	das Rührei	*dass ruehrai*
screw	die Schraube	*dee shrowber*
screwdriver	der Schraubenzieher	*shrowben-tseeher*
sculpture	die Bildhauerei	*dee bilt-hower-rai*
sea	die See/das Meer	*dee zay/dass meer*
seasick	seekrank	*zaykrank*
seat	der Platz/der Sitzplatz	*dayr plats/dayr zitsplats*
seat belt	der Gurt	*dayr goort*
seat reservation	die Platzkarte	*dee platskarter*
second	die Sekunde	*dee zekoonder*
second (number)	zweite	*tsvaiter*
second-hand	gebraucht	*gebrowkht*
sedative	das Beruhigúngsmittel	*dass berooee-goongz-mittel*
see (to)	sehen	*zayhen*
see (to) (view)	sich ansehen/besichtigen	*anzayhen/besikhtigen*
self-timer	der Selbstauslöser	*dayr zelpst-ows-loezer*
send	(ver)schicken	*(fair)shikken*
sentence	der Satz	*dayr zats*
September	der September	*dayr zeptember*
serious	ernst	*ayrnst*
service	die Bedienung	*dee bedeenoong*
serviette	die Serviette	*dee zairveeyeter*
sewing thread	das Nähgarn	*dass naygarn*
shade	der Schatten	*dayr shatten*
shallow	flach	*flakh*
shampoo	das Shampoo	*dass shampoo*
shark	der Hai	*dayr hai*
shave	rasieren	*razeeren*
shaver	der Rasierapparat	*dayr razeer-apparart*
shaving brush	der Rasierpinsel	*dayr razeer-pinzel*
shaving soap	die Rasierseife	*dee razeer-zaifer*
sheet	das Laken	*dass larken*
sherry	der Sherry	*dayr sherry*

shirt	das (Ober)hemd	*dass (oaber)hemt*
shoe	der Schuh	*dayr shoo*
shoe polish	die Schuhcreme	*dee shookraymer*
shoe shop	das Schuhgeschäft	*dass shoogesheft*
shoemaker	der Schuhmacher/ Schuster	*dayr shoomakher/ shooster*
shoes (mountaineering)	die Bergschuhe	*dee bayrk-shooer*
shop (vb.)	einkaufen/einholen	*ainkowfen/ainhoalen*
shop	der Laden	*dayr larden*
shop assistant	die Verkäuferin	*dee fayrkoyferin*
shop window	das Schaufenster	*dass showfenster*
shopping centre	das Einkaufszentrum	*dass ainkowfs-tsentroom*
short	kurz	*koorts*
short circuit	der Kurzschluss	*dayr koorts-shlooss*
shorts	die kurze Hosen	*dee koortser-hoazen*
shoulder	die Schulter	*dee shoolter*
show	die Show/die Schau	*dee shoa/dee show*
shower	die Dusche	*dee doosher*
shutter	der Auslöser	*dayr owsloezer*
side	die Seite	*dee zaiter*
sieve	das Sieb	*dass zeep*
sign	unterschreiben	*oontershraiben*
sign	das Schild	*dass shilt*
signature	die Unterschrift	*dee oonter-shrift*
silence	die Stille	*dee shtiller*
silver	das Silber	*dass zilber*
silver-plated	versilbert	*fayrzilbert*
simple	einfach	*ainfakh*
single (unmarried)	unverheiratet/ledig	*oonfayrhai-rartet/laydikh*
single	Einzel-	*aintsel-*
single (ticket)	einfach	*ainfakh*
sir	mein Herr	*main hayr*
sister	die Schwester	*dee shvester*
sit	sitzen	*zitsen*
sit down	sich setzen	*zikh zetsen*
size	die Grösse	*dee groersser*

ski	Ski fahren/laufen	sheefahren/lowfen
ski boots	Skischuhe	sheeshooer
ski goggles	die Skibrille	dee sheebriller
ski instructor	der Skilehrer	dayr sheelairer
ski lessons/class	die Skistunde(n)	dee sheeshtoonder(n)
ski lift	der Skilift	dayr sheelift
ski pants	die Skihose	dee sheehoazer
ski pass	der Skipass	dayr sheepass
ski slope	die Skipiste	dee sheepister
ski stick	der Skistock	dayr sheeshtok
ski suit	der Skianzug	dayr sheeantsook
ski wax	das Skiwachs	dass sheevakhs
skiing	der Langlauf	dayr langlowf
(cross-country)		
skimmed	halbfett	halpfett
skin	die Haut	dee howt
skirt	der Rock	dayr rock
skis	die Skier	dee sheeyer
skis (cross-country)	die Laufskier	dee lowf-sheeyer
sleep	schlafen	shlarfen
sleeping car	der Schlafwagen	dayr shlarfvargen
sleeping pills	die Schlaftabletten	dee shlarf-tabletten
slide	das Dia	dass deear
slip	der Unterrock	dayr oonterrock
slip road	die Auffahrt	dee owffahrt
slow	langsam	langzarm
slow train	der Nahverkehrszug	dayr narfayrkairs-tsook
small	klein	klain
small change	das Wechselgeld	dass vekhselgelt
small change	das Kleingeld	dass klaingelt
smell	stinken	shtinken
smoke	der Rauch	dayr rowkh
smoke (vb.)	rauchen	rowkhen
smoked	geräuchert	geroykhert
smoking	das Raucherabteil	dass rowkher aptail
compartment		
snake	die Schlange	dee shlanger

snorkel	der Schnorchel	*dayr shnorkhel*
snow (verb)	schneien	*shnaien*
snow	der Schnee	*dayr shnay*
snow chains	die Schneekette	*dee shnay-ketter*
soap	die Seife	*dee zaifer*
soap box	die Seifenschachtel	*dee zaifen-shakhtel*
soap powder	das Seifenpulver	*dass zaifen-pullfer*
socket	die Steckdose	*dee shtekdoazer*
socks	die Socken	*dee zokken*
soft drink	das Erfrischungs-	*dass ayrfrishoongs-*
	getränk	*getrenk*
sole (fish)	die (See)zunge	*dee (zay)tsoonger*
sole	die Sohle	*dee zoaler*
solicitor	der Rechtsanwalt	*dayr rekhts-anvalt*
someone	jemand	*yaymant*
sometimes	manchmal	*manshmarl*
somewhere	irgendwo	*eergentvo*
son	der Sohn	*dayr zoan*
soon	bald	*barlt*
sorbet	das Sorbet	*dass sorbay*
sore	das Geschwür	*dass geshvuer*
sore throat	die Halsschmerzen	*dee halz-shmayrtsen*
sorry	Entschuldigung/	*entshool-deegoong/*
	Verzeihung	*fayrtsayoong*
sort	die Sorte	*dee zorter*
soup	die Suppe	*dee zoopper*
sour	sauer	*zower*
sour cream	der Sauerrahm	*dayr zowerrarm*
source	die Quelle	*dee kveller*
south	der Süden	*dayr zueden*
souvenir	das Andenken/das	*dass andenken/dass*
	Souvenir	*zooveneer*
spaghetti	die Spaghetti	*dee shpagetti*
spanner	der Gabelschlüssel	*dayr garbel-shluessel*
(open-ended)		
spanner	der Mutternschlüssel	*dayr muttern-shluesell*
spare	die Reserve	*dee rezayrver*

spare parts	die Ersatzteile	dee erzats-tailer
spare tyre	der Reservereifen	dayr rezayrver-raifen
spare wheel	das Reserverad	dass rezayrverrart
speak	sprechen	shprekhen
special	besonders	bezonderz
specialist	der Spezialist/ der Facharzt	dayr shpetseealist/dayr fakhartst
speciality	die Spezialität	dee shpetseea-lee-tayt
speed limit	die Höchst-geschwindigkeit	dee hoekhst geshvindikh-kait
spell	buchstabieren	bookh-shtarbee-ren
spicy	gewürzt	gewuertst
splinter	der Splitter	dayr shplitter
spoon	der Löffel	dayr loeffel
sport	der Sport	dayr shport
sports (to do)	Sport treiben	shport traiben
sports centre	die Sporthalle	dee shporthaller
spot	der Platz/Ort	dayr plats/dayr ort
sprain	verstauchen	fayrshtowkhen
spring	der Frühling	dayr fruehling
square (place)	der Platz	dayr plats
square	quadratisch	kvadrartish
squash	das Squash	dass skvash
stadium	das Stadion	dass shtadeeon
stain	der Fleck	dayr flek
stain remover	das Fleckenmittel	dass flekken-mittel
stairs	die Treppe	dee trepper
stalls	das Parkett	dass parkett
stamp	die Briefmarke	dee breefmarker
start	starten/anlassen	shtarten/anlassen
station	der Bahnhof	dayr barnhoaf
statue	das Standbild/das Denkmal	dass shtantbilt/ dass denkmarl
stay (vb.)	bleiben/ wohnen	blaiben/voanen
stay	der Aufenthalt	dayr owfenthalt
steal	stehlen	shtaylen
steel (stainless)	der (rostfreie) Stahl	dayr (rosstfraier) shtarl

stench	der Gestank	*dayr geshtank*
sting	stechen	*shtekhen*
stitch (med)	nähen	*nayhen*
stock	die Brühe	*dee brueher*
stockings	die Strümpfe	*dee shtruempfer*
stomach	der Magen/der Bauch	*dayr margen/dayr bowkh*
stomach ache	die Magenschmerzen/	*dee margen-shmayrtsen/*
	die Bauchschmerzen	*dee bowkh-shmayrtsen*
stomach cramps	die Bauchkrämpfe	*dee bowkh-krempfer*
stools	der Stuhl(gang)	*dayr shtool(gang)*
stop	halten	*halten*
stop	die Haltestelle	*dee halter-shteller*
stopover	die Zwischenlandung	*dee tsvishen-landoong*
storm	stürmen	*shtuermen*
storm	der Sturm	*dayr shtoorm*
straight (hair)	glatt(es Haar)	*glatt(ez har)*
straight ahead	geradeaus	*gerarderows*
straw	der Trinkhalm	*dayr trinkhalm*
strawberries	die Erdbeeren	*dee ayrtbeeren*
street	die Strasse	*dee shtrasser*
street side	die Strassenseite	*dee shtrarssen-zaiter*
strike	der Streik	*dayr shtraik*
study	studieren	*shtoodeeren*
subtitled	untertitelt	*oonterteetelt*
succeed	glücken	*gluekken*
sugar	der Zucker	*dayr tsooker*
suit	der Anzug	*dayr antsook*
suitcase	der Koffer	*dayr koffer*
summer	der Sommer	*dayr zommer*
summertime	die Sommerzeit	*dee zommertsait*
sun	die Sonne	*dee zonner*
sun hat	der Sonnenhut	*dayr zonnenhoot*
sunbathe	sich sonnen	*zikh zonnen*
Sunday	der Sonntag	*dayr zonntark*
sunglasses	die Sonnenbrille	*dee zonnenbriller*
sunrise	der Sonnenaufgang	*dayr zonnen-owf-gang*
sunset	der Sonnenuntergang	*dayr zonnen-oonter-gang*

sunstroke	der Sonnenstich	*dayr zonnenshtikh*
suntan lotion	die Sonnen(schutz)-creme	*dee zonnen(shoots) kraymer*
suntan oil	das Sonnen(schutz)öl	*dass zonnen(shoots)oel*
supermarket	der Supermarkt	*dayr zooper markt*
surcharge	der Zuschlag	*dayr tsooshlark*
surf	surfen	*zoorfen*
surf board	das Surfbrett	*dass zoorfbrett*
surgery	die Sprechstunde	*dee shprekh-shtoonder*
surname	der Nachname	*dayr nakhnarmer*
surprise	die Überraschung	*dee ueber-rashoong*
swallow (vb.)	runterschlucken	*roonter-shlooken*
swamp	der Sumpf	*dayr zoompf*
sweat	der Schweiss	*dayr shvaiss*
sweet (a)	das Bonbon	*dass bonbon*
sweet (nice)	lieb	*leep*
sweet (sugary)	süss	*zuess*
sweetcorn	der Mais	*dayr maiss*
sweetener	der Süßstoff	*dayr zuess-shtoff*
sweets	Süssigkeiten	*zuessikh-kaiten*
swim	schwimmen/baden	*shvimmen/bardern*
swimming pool	das Schwimmbad/die Badeanstalt (spa)	*dass shvimmbart/dee barder-anshtalt*
swimming trunks	die Badehose	*dee barder-hoazer*
swindle	der Betrug	*dayr betrook*
switch	der Schalter	*dayr shalter*
synagogue	die Synagoge	*dee zuena-goager*

T

table	der Tisch	*dayr tish*
table tennis	das Tischtennis	*dass tishtennis*
tablet	die Tablette	*dee tabletter*
take	nehmen	*naymen*
take (time)	dauern	*dowern*
take pictures	fotografieren	*foto-grafeerren*

talcum powder	der Talkpuder	*dass talkpooder*
talk	reden	*rayden*
tampons	die Tampons	*dee tampons*
tap	der (Wasser)hahn	*dayr (vasser)harn*
tap water	das Leitungswasser	*dass laitoongs-vasser*
taste	probieren	*probeeren*
tax free shop	der Taxfree-Shop	*dayr taksfree-shop*
taxi	das Taxi	*dass tarksi*
taxi stand	der Taxistand	*dayr tarksishtant*
tea	der Tee	*dayr tay*
teapot	die Teekanne	*dee taykanner*
teaspoon	der Teelöffel	*dayr tay-loeffell*
telephone (by)	telefonisch	*taylayfoanish*
television	der Fernseher	*dayr fayrnzayer*
temperature	die Temperatur	*dee temperatoor*
temporary filling	die Notfüllung	*dee noatfueloong*
tender	zart	*tsart*
tennis	das Tennis	*dass tennis*
tennis ball	der Tennisball	*dayr tennisbarl*
tennis court	der Tennisplatz	*dayr tennisplats*
tennis racket	der Tennisschläger	*dayr tennis-shlayger*
tent	das Zelt	*dass tselt*
tent peg	der (Zelt)hering	*dayr (tselt)hayring*
terrace	die Terrasse	*dee terasser*
terribly	entsetzlich	*entzetslikh*
thank	danken, sich bedanken	*danken, zikh bedanken*
thank you	vielen Dank	*feelen dank*
thaw	tauen	*towen*
the day after tomorrow	übermorgen	*ueber morgen*
theatre	das Theater	*dass tayarter*
theft	der Diebstahl	*dayr deepshtarl*
there	da/dort	*da/dort*
thermal bath	das Thermalbad	*dass termarlbart*
thermometer	das Thermometer	*dass termomayter*
thick	dick	*dik*
thief	der Dieb	*dayr deep*

thigh	der Oberschenkel	*dayr oaber-shenkel*
thin	dünn/mager	*duenn/marger*
things	die Sachen	*dee zakhen*
think	denken	*denken*
third	das Drittel	*dass drittel*
thirst	der Durst	*dayr doorst*
this afternoon	heute nachmittag	*hoyter nakhmittark*
this evening	heute abend	*hoyter arbent*
this morning	heute morgen	*hoyter morgen*
thread	der Faden/das Garn	*dayr farden/dass garn*
throat	die Kehle	*dee kayler*
throat lozenges	die Halstabletten	*dee hals-tablet-ten*
throw up	(sich) erbrechen	*(zikh) ayrbrekhen*
thunderstorm	das Gewitter	*dass gevitter*
Thursday	der Donnerstag	*dayr donnerstark*
ticket (admission)	die (Eintritts)karte	*dee (aintritts)karter*
ticket (travel)	die (Fahr)karte	*dee (far)karter*
ticket	das Ticket	*dass ticket*
tie	die Krawatte	*dee kravatter*
tights	die Strumpfhose	*dee shtroompf-hoazer*
time	die Zeit	*dee tsait*
timetable	der Fahrplan	*dayr farplan*
tin	die Dose/die Büchse	*dee doazer/de buekhser*
tip	das Trinkgeld	*dass trinkgelt*
tissues	Papiertaschentücher	*papeer-tashen-tuekher*
toast	das Toastbrot	*dass toastbroat*
tobacco	der Tabak	*dayr tabak*
tobacconist's	der Tabakladen/	*dayr tabaklarden*
	die (Tabak)	*dayr tabaklarden*
	trafik (Aus.)	*dee (tabak) trafeek*
toboggan	der Schlitten	*dayr shlitten*
today	heute	*hoyter*
toe	der Zeh/die Zehe	*dayr tsay/dee tsayer*
together	zusammen	*tsoozammen*
toilet	die Toilette/das W.C.	*dee twarletter/dass vaytsay*
toilet paper	das Toilettenpapier	*dass twarletten-papeer*
216 toiletries	die Toilettenartikel	*dee twarletten arteekel*

tomato	die Tomate	*dee tomarter*
tomato purée	das Tomatenmark	*dass tomarten mark*
tomato sauce	der Tomatenketchup	*dayr tomarten ketchup*
tomorrow	morgen	*morgen*
tongue	die Zunge	*dee tsoonger*
tonic water	das Tonic	*dass toanik*
tonight	heute nacht	*hoyter nakht*
too much	zuviel	*tsoofeel*
tool	das Werkzeug	*dass vayrktsoyk*
tooth	der Zahn	*dayr tsarn*
toothache	die Zahnschmerzen	*dee tsarnshmayrtsen*
toothbrush	die Zahnbürste	*dee tsarnbuerster*
toothpaste	die Zahnpasta	*dee tsarnpaster*
toothpick	der Zahnstocher	*dayr tsarnshtokher*
top up	nachfüllen	*nakhfuellen*
total	total/insgesamt	*totarl/insgezamt*
tough	zäh	*tsay*
tour	die Rundreise	*dee roontraizer*
tour guide	der Reiseführer	*dayr raizerfuerer*
tourist card	die Touristenkarte	*dee tooristen karter*
tourist class	die Touristenklasse	*dee tooristen klasser*
Tourist Information Office	das Fremdenverkehrs büro	*dass fremden fayrkayrz buero*
tourist menu	das Touristenmenü	*dass tooristen-menue*
tow	(ab)schleppen	*(ap)shleppen*
tow cable	das (Ab)schleppseil	*dass (ap)shlepzail*
towel	das Handtuch	*dass hanttookh*
tower	der Turm	*dayr toorm*
town	die Stadt	*dee shtatt*
town hall	das Rathaus	*dass rarthowz*
town walk	der Stadtrundgang	*dayr shtatroontgang*
toy	das Spielzeug	*dass shpeeltsoyk*
traffic	der Verkehr	*dayr fayrkayr*
traffic light	die Verkehrsampel	*dee fayrkayrs-ampel*
train	der Zug	*dayr tsook*
train ticket	die Fahr-/Bahnkarte	*dee far-/barnkarter*
train timetable	der Fahrplan	*dayr farplarn*

trainers	die Sportschuhe	*dee shportshooer*
translate	übersetzen	*ueber zetsen*
travel	reisen	*raizen*
travel agent	das Reisebüro	*dass raizer-buero*
travel guide	der Reiseführer	*dayr raizerfuerer*
traveller	der/die Reisende	*dayr/dee raizender*
traveller's cheque	der Reisescheck	*dayr raizershek*
treacle/syrup	der Sirup	*dayr zeeroop*
treatment	die Behandlung	*dee behandloong*
triangle	das Dreieck	*dass draiek*
trim	kürzen	*kuertsen*
trip	der Ausflug/die Reise	*dayr owsflook/dee raizer*
trouble	die Beschwerde	*dee beshverder*
trout	die Forelle	*dee foreller*
trunk code	die Vorwahl	*dee forvarl*
try on	anprobieren	*anprobeeren*
tube (inner)	der Schlauch	*dayr shlowkh*
tube	die Tube	*dee toober*
Tuesday	der Dienstag	*dayr deenstark*
tumble drier	der Trockner	*dayr trokner*
tuna	der Thunfisch	*dayr toonfish*
tunnel	der Tunnel	*dayr toonnel*
turn	das Mal	*dass marl*
TV	das T.V./Fernsehen	*dass tayfow/fayrn-zayhen*
tweezers	die Pinzette	*dee pintsetter*
tyre	der Reifen	*dayr raifen*
tyre lever	der Reifenheber	*dayr raifen-hayber*
tyre pressure	die Reifenspannung	*dee raifen-shpannoong*

U

ugly	hässlich	*hesslikh*
umbrella	der Regenschirm	*dayr raygensheerm*
under	unten	*oonten*
underground (train)	die U-Bahn	*dee oo-barn*

underground railway system	das U-Bahnnetz	dass oo-barnnets
underground station	die U-Bahnhaltestelle	dee oo-barn-halter-shteller
underpants	die Unterhose	dee oonterhoazer
understand	begreifen	begraifen
underwear	die Unterwäsche	dee oontervesher
undress	sich freimachen/(gen.) sich ausziehen	zikh fraimakhen/ zikh owstseehen
unemployed	arbeitslos	arbaitsloas
uneven	ungleichmässig	oon-glaikh-mayssig
university	die Universität	dee oonee-vayrsee-tayt
unleaded (petrol)	bleifrei	blaifrai
up	nach oben	nakh oben
urgency	die Eile	dee ailer
urgent	dringend	dringent
urine	der Harn	dayr harn
usually	meistens	maistens

V

vacate	räumen	roymen
vaccinate	impfen	impfen
vagina	die Vagina	dee vageena
vaginal infection	die Scheidenentzündung	dee shaiden-ent-tsuen doong
valid	gültig	gueltikh
valley	das Tal	dass tarl
valuable	wertvoll	vayrtfoll
van	der Lieferwagen	dayr leefer-vargen
vanilla	die Vanille	dee vaniller
vase	die Vase	dee varzer
vaseline	die Vaseline	dee vasseleener
veal	das Kalbfleisch	dass kalpflaish
vegetable soup	die Gemüsesuppe	dee gemuezer-zupper
vegetables	das Gemüse	dass gemuezer

vegetarian	der Vegetarier	*dayr vegetareeyar*
vein	die Ader	*dee arder*
venereal disease	die Geschlechtskrankheit	*dee geshlekhts-krank-hait*
via	über	*ueber*
view	die Aussicht	*dee owszikht*
village	das Dorf	*dass dorf*
visa	das Visum	*dass veezum*
visit (verb)	besuchen	*bezookhen*
visit	der Besuch	*dayr bezookh*
vitamin	das Vitamin	*dass vitameen*
vitamin tablets	Vitamintabletten	*vitameen-tabletten*
volleyball	der Volleyball	*dayr volleyball*
vomit	sich erbrechen	*zikh erbrekhen*

W

wait	warten	*varten*
waiter	der Ober	*dayr oaber*
waiting room	das Wartezimmer	*dass varter-tsimmer*
waitress	die Kellnerin/ die Serviererin	*dee kelnerin/ dee zayrveererin*
wake up	wecken	*vekken*
Wales	Wales	*vaylz*
walk	der Spaziergang	*dayr shpatseer-gang*
walk (vb.)	spazierengehen	*shpatseeren-gayhen*
wallet	die Brieftasche	*dee breeftasher*
wardrobe	der Kleiderschrank	*dayr klaider-shrank*
warm	warm	*varm*
warn	warnen	*varnen*
warning	die Warnung	*dee varnoong*
warning triangle	das Warndreieck	*dass varn-draieck*
wash	waschen	*vashen*
washing	die Wäsche	*dee vesher*
washing line	die Wäscheleine	*dee vesher-lainer*
washing machine	die Waschmaschine	*dee vashmasheener*

washing-powder	das Waschmittel	dass vashmittel
wasp	die Wespe	dee vesper
water	das Wasser	dass vasser
water ski	das Wasserski	dass vassershee
waterproof	wasserdicht	vasserdikht
wave	die Welle	dee veller
wave-pool	das Wellenbad	dass vellenbart
way	die Weise	dee vaizer
way (path)	der Weg	dayr vayk
we	wir	veer
weak	schwach	shvakh
weather	das Wetter	dass vetter
weather forecast	der Wetterbericht	dayr vetter-berikht
wedding	die Hochzeit	dee hokhtsait
Wednesday	der Mittwoch	dayr mitvokh
week	die Woche	dee vokher
weekend	das Wochenende	dass vokhen-ender
weekend duty	der Notdienst	dayr noatdeenst
weekly ticket	die Wochenkarte	dee vokhen-karter
welcome	willkommen	villkommen
well	gut	goot
west	der Westen	dayr vesten
wet	nass	nass
what	was	vass
wheel	das Rad	dass rart
wheelchair	der Rollstuhl	dayr rollshtool
when	wann	van
where	wo	vo
which	welch-(-e,-er,-es)	velkh-(-e,-er,-es)
whipped cream	die Schlagsahne/	dee shlarkzarner/
	der Schlagrahm/	der shlarkrarm
	das Schlagobers	dass shlarkoberz
	(Aus.)	
white	weiss	vaiss
who	wer	vayr
wholemeal	das Vollkorn	dass follkorn
wholemeal bread	das Vollkornbrot	dass follkornbroat

why	warum	*vahroom*
widow	die Witwe	*dee vitveh*
widower	der Witwer	*dayr vitver*
wife	die Frau	*dee frow*
wind	der Wind	*dayr vint*
windbreak	der Windschutz	*dayr vintshoots*
window	das Fenster	*dass fenster*
windscreen wiper	der Scheibenwischer	*dayr shaiben-visher*
wine	der Wein	*dayr vain*
winter	der Winter	*dayr vinter*
witness	der Zeuge	*dayr tsoyger*
wonderful	herrlich	*hayrlikh*
wood	das Holz	*dass holts*
wool	die Wolle	*dee voller*
word	das Wort	*dass vort*
work	die Arbeit	*dee arbait*
working day	der Werktag/	*dayr arbaits/dayr vayrktark*
	der Arbeits-	
worn	abgenutzt	*apgenootst*
worried	beunruhigt	*be-oonroo-ikht*
wound	die Wunde	*dee vunder*
wrap (gift)	einpacken	*ainpakken*
wrist	das Handgelenk	*dass hantgelenk*
write	schreiben	*shraiben*
write down	aufschreiben	*owfshraiben*
written	schriftlich	*shriftlikh*
wrong	falsch/verkehrt	*falsh/fayrkayrt*

Y

yacht	die Yacht	*dee yakht*
year	das Jahr	*dass yahr*
yellow	gelb	*gelp*
yes	ja	*yar*
yesterday	gestern	*gestern*
yoghurt	der/das Joghurt (Aus.)	*dayr/dass yoghoort*
you (polite)	Sie	*zee*
you too	gleichfalls	*glaikhfals*
youth hostel	die Jugendherberge	*dee yoogent-hayr-bayrger*

Z

zebra crossing	der Zebrastreifen	*dayr tsebra-shtraifen*
zip	der Reissverschluss	*dayr raiss-fayr-shlooss*
zoo	der Zoo	*dayr tsoo*